Jeff Bezos: The Force Behind the Brand

Jeff Bezos: The Force Behind the Brand

Insight and Analysis into the Life and Accomplishments of the Richest Man on the Planet

JR MacGregor

Jeff Bezos: The Force Behind the Brand

Insight and Analysis into the Life and Accomplishments of the Richest Man on the Planet

Published by CAC Publishing LLC.

ISBN 978-1-948489-09-6 paperback

ISBN 978-1-948489-10-2 eBook

This book is dedicated to those that dream of changing the world.

Make sure to check out the next book in this 'Billionaire Visionaries' series:

Elon Musk: Moving the World One Technology at a Time

Table of Contents

Preface

Despite our better angels, we seem to do things without rhyme nor apparent reason. We peer out at our neighbor's new car; we inflict our political views on our family; we judge others by the standards we set arbitrarily for ourselves, and we can't get enough of reality TV. All these factors of the human profile are connected more intricately than we realize.

We do these things because the human species is inextricably connected at a very deep level and the way it manifests is in our curiosity of our fellow man. We are all gifted in our own way but, more often than not, we do not know how to understand our gifts or use them in a way that results in spectacular results.

We don't know how to be our own Elon Musk, or our own Bill Gates, Steve Jobs or Jeff Bezos. All these men (just a short sampling of some of the achievers out there) are extremely successful in what they do, yet there is no duplicate among them. Bezos achieved tremendous success doing something very different to Steve Jobs. Bill Gates contributed something very different – and went about doing it very differently from Elon Musk. But they all contributed significantly and in diverse areas of the life that our species experiences.

We are not looking and, really, we shouldn't be looking to do what they did, but we are looking to understand ourselves in the way they understood themselves and exploited their better angels.

Let me illustrate.

In writing this book about Bezos, I learned so many things about him but, more importantly, I learned something very important about my youngest son who behaves a lot like Bezos did when he was still a kid. As I researched his life, the avalanche of anecdotes that I pieced together in my research – while supposed to paint a picture of Bezos in my head so that I could narrate it for all of you, ended up painting a picture of my youngest son. And that changed my view of him and how I respond to him because it taught me how to understand my youngest better – who has always been a skosh different from typical kids. I don't expect you to do that with your kids, but it could help you explain something about yourself and if you develop that further, who knows where that may lead.

I'll say it here and I will say it again later, biographies are never about the subject and its gossip value. Biographies of great achievers are about ourselves. If you see it in that light, then you are forced to see the good in others so that you can find the power and strength in yourself.

It's a good thing that Bezos is in the news as much as he is and that has created a buzz about him, because the lessons that he can teach us just by dissecting his experience and observing his trajectory will be of huge benefit to large swaths of people – not everyone though. Some of you may get more benefit from Jack Ma; others may get more out of learning about Albert Einstein. My only hope is that my humble attempt at piecing together a small sampling of his interesting life and accomplishments plays a role in touching your life and making it better.

We all have a little voice in our head that can cause success or chaos. If we finetune that voice, it will alert us to things that will catapult us into the realm of our needs and desires. If we trip and start heeding the wrong voice, then we will start to act on our fears and biases. This book is not about choosing which voice you pick but is about a man that has so finely tuned his senses that he knows exactly which voice is telling him what and knows when to listen to it. It is not something that comes from meticulous and articulate definition, but rather comes from mistakes, reflections, more mistakes, learning, and still more mistakes and then, after all the challenges have been surmounted, all the problems solved, and all the mountains climbed, we find achievement on the horizon, and success in the dawn.

Introduction

Let me state up front that you will not see a bad word written about this man in this book. But that is not because this book is written as an adulation to the current wealthiest man on the planet.

Instead, it is written this way because we cannot hope to emulate or learn from a man – any man or woman for that matter – that we are mocking or finding fault with. Biographies are not about the subject of the book. Biographies are about the person reading it, and their quest to find the spark that is within them. Not about paying homage to the subject of the biography.

However, it is easy to get carried away in the evolving narrative of who the person is behind the name. It becomes complex to decipher the man behind the company, and the brain behind the idea. And that is, after all, why we are intrigued by this person – his character, his actions, his reasoning. He is interesting because of his achievement, and the string of ideas, decisions, and actions he has taken to arrive at where he is at this point in time.

This is also not a book about the rights and wrongs, the vices and virtues, or the ethical or brazen business moves that may or may not impact others. Again, this is about the trek and the soul of a man combined with his chutzpah to make something, see something, perfect something, that is better than anyone else has to that point. There are things you can say about Bill Gates, or about Steve Jobs, Jack Ma, Richard Branson and anyone who has reached a certain level of success that is beyond what most others have dreamed of doing. But judging them will not get you far.

When it comes to Bezos (by the way it's pronounced 'Bay-Zos,' not Bee Zos) there are a lot of you who are going to say that he did this or did that and put this company or that company out of business. I understand your sense of empathy for the vanquished and those companies that got hit and shuttered, or the companies that had to downsize because of the rise of Amazon. For instance, the likes of Barnes and Noble – which is especially ironic, since it was the coffee shop in Barnes and Noble that played host to Bezos and his compadres, as well as their early customers and investors in Seattle. It's not just Barnes and Noble that hit a brick wall when Amazon started to rise; it was retailers like Macy's and Nordstroms as well. But it also doesn't just stop at brick and mortar companies in old tech – it's new tech as well. Etsy, for example, has also seen better days.

For those of you who cast Amazon and, by extension, Jeff Bezos as evil and un-American (talk of monopoly and all that), I urge you to think again. Have you played that thought out in your head – do you really think that they are out to destroy the past icons of American commerce because they have nothing better to do? No. That is the genius of Amazon and the brilliance of Bezos. They are out to revolutionize the landscape and take advantage of technology in doing so.

Or maybe you think it has to do with greed at the expense of others? I don't see any evidence of that. What I see is a person who has identified a piece of technology and used that technology in ways others are only now starting to comprehend.

As the book unfolds, one of the things that you will start to understand about Bezos is that there are two sides to him (more actually but, in this instance, these two sides are in stark contrast with each other.) On the one side you have a man who is so tech savvy that he sees their utility in the nitty-gritty of the infrastructure (of that technology) – he is the kind of guy who could tell you why the Starship Enterprise can go into warp and why it maxes out at Warp 9 – by the way, if you look closely, Bezos has a cameo appearance as one of the alien characters in Star Trek Beyond (you should totally look that up). The other side of him is one that is almost stoic in a philosophical way. He is one of those people that reads new-age authors in philosophy like Taleb (Nassim Nicholas) and other technology philosophers. He is one of those people that sees the fundamental thread that runs through things and he can't really understand the perspective of those who do not see that as well. He is highly intolerant of ignorance.

His ability to understand the place for technology in today's world is because of his philosophical mental framework and his understanding of how things play out.

Bezos is not caught up in his money the way we are and, if you really want to understand the secret of his success, you need to leave your preconceived notions of fair play, arbitrary standards of moral right and wrong, ethical standards of business, and antiquated notions of competitive forces right here before you move forward.

When you do that, what I assure you that you will find is the secret sauce that is packed into all things that Bezos touches. It is not for the faint of heart.

The best way to chop up and consume a biography (any biography – not just this one) is to look at the cause and effect of a person's actions as it pertains to themselves and the world around them. When you look at someone like Bill Gates, do you turn around and discount all the philanthropy he has done, all the wealth he has amassed, and all the benefits that have come from his building of Microsoft? Or do you look at the possibly unfair (I don't think it's unfair – but many who judge think that it is) way that he got the source code for the original version of DOS? He did what he did and changed the world in the wake of that decision.

We are all the sum of our choices, as Bezos said in his speech to the kids at Stanford during the commencement ceremony – and rightfully so. We have to live and die by our decisions and how that affects all things in our gravity. How we do them and what we do comes from those choices and those decisions. If we choose to take the path that people like Bezos or Gates have taken, then the outcome will be pretty close to the same. It's like baking a cake – if you follow the exact measurements and the correct sequence and methods, you're going to come pretty close to the same result. The chance of getting that result is also whether you are doing it willingly or just going through the motions. I can tell you from personal experience that if you go through the motions but don't really believe in it, then you're wasting your time.

But if you want to strike at the chance for success and contribute toward the trajectory of this civilization, then you gotta get up and break some eggs and you should watch attentively how some of these masters go about achieving their success so that you can do the same – in your own field. I would like to think that is why you are reading this biography.

That is how it is written – not just to give you salacious juicy facts and figures, but to highlight the junctions and events that brought about decisions that charted a meteoric path. It is a fascinating story and one that has taught me so much. It is a quest that transcends space, time, and person.

To aid that quest, as I have said, it is best not to highlight the negatives, or focus on the subject's errors (in essence, reserve opinion and judgment of the subject and look for the constructive contributions). Rather, it is best to look at the challenges, ask the questions, digest the reasoning, and contemplate the similarities.

We all need direction and clarity to go about achieving the various vocations that we are drawn to. We all need ideas and we all need examples to do the things we would like to do but hesitate to because subconsciously we do not have a clear path ahead.

Not all of us. In fact, only very few of us who read this book, and go on to read other books about Bezos, and books about other men of significant accomplishment, will go out and successfully build another Amazon or build the replacement of

Amazon. But that is not what I envision as I write this book. What I envision is that all of you find your own spark and do the things that light up your soul. For Bezos, it was technology (I will come to that in the next chapter). For Steve Jobs it was elegance. For Bill Gates, it was mass markets and technology adoption. For Jack Ma, it was advancing Chinese businesses.

You will not find the answer to your pressing and subconscious questions of life and how to succeed by just reading one book (or many books) about one man. You will come close when you read about many. Ultimately, your success already lies within you. You can't copy another person's success; you can only understand the frame of their mind and see what makes things tick, then learn to bring your own powers to bear in your own life.

In light of this, I hope that you are inspired by the facts, anecdotes, and analysis contained in this book. I hope that you find your own spark that propels you to the next level. I pray that you evolve into your full potential and touch all those within your gravity to achieve the same.

***

Chapter 1 An Overview

"Invention is by its very nature disruptive. If you want to be understood at all times, then don't do anything new."

At the time of publishing, Amazon's share price stands at $1,450 per share, giving it a total market capitalization of 699 Billion Dollars. This puts Amazon in the top 20 largest global companies. As large as it is, it is not the largest company in the world just yet. That title belongs to PetroChina, which is valued at over 10 Trillion Dollars – but things like PetroChina don't count in this calculus as those are state-run companies and, thus, do not detract from the size and achievement of our own Amazon.

In the US, Amazon is the fourth largest with those numbers, just barely behind Apple, Google, and

Microsoft. Most people would tell you that Amazon started as a bookseller and that was the goal all along. It's not.

Amazon's first products were books indeed, but it wasn't the founder's idea that that would be the be-all-end-all of Amazon. He knew from the very beginning that it was the juxtaposition of technology and utility that he wanted to exploit – not just books. He didn't think about selling books as his purpose in life.

There are two things wrong with this picture. The first is that it casts Bezos as a simpleton – which he is not; he is as complex as they come. Second, it makes it look like Amazon's success was by accident – it was not. It was deliberate, calculated and chiseled into its present form.

Start with Books

We all know that he started with books from his garage in Seattle – where he had just moved to from New York. Amazon was best known for that, and even still today, Amazon remains the largest bookseller in the world even though it has stopped labeling itself as such, as it did in 1994.

The decision to start with books back in 1994, was because books happened to be the one item in mail order catalogs that lent itself to online purchase and shipping. You will see later in the book that Bezos had thought long and hard about what product to offer in this new world of the Internet and so he looked through all the possible goods and services that could be catalogued and sold; and he found that the reason books were not part of the mail-order business was because there were so many titles that no one could possibly print a catalogue and send it to every household via US Post. The Internet solved that problem, naturally, and it was the easiest way that Bezos could enter the world of e-commerce. He already had the ideal medium, now he needed the perfect product – and he found it.

That is not always the easiest thing to do if you think about it. We get to sit back and say that it was an obvious choice but, if you really think about it, how often can someone say they looked at something and managed to find an opportunity within it? It is the result of a resourceful brain – it's like being MacGyver in the business world.

The Technology

Think about that for a minute and you will realize that, while the Internet has successfully eclipsed the mail order world that preceded it, the mail-order business was a huge industry. Remember the loads of junk mail that you used to receive, pre-90s? Remember the catalogs that used to fill up your mailbox? At the heart of that was commerce. At the heart of that was the seller reaching out to a buyer and letting them know that they had stuff to sell.

When Amazon started in the mind of this young electrical engineer in the offices of a Wall Street quantitative hedge-fund house, it wasn't because he thought mail order was a great business. He did so because he believed that the Internet was a great channel to reach millions of people.

Most companies look at their product then think about the distribution channel. Fair enough. But no one thinks about the channel and then tries to stuff it with product. Yet, that is what Amazon is the result of.

That's all it was – an entry point; a wedge to leverage the new network of distribution. It would be like picking up the latest technology in graphenes and saying, "OK, now that I've got it what can I do to fully take advantage of this?"

By no means was Amazon the first to try selling books online either. There were already a few Internet companies that had started to offer books online. And we will get to that but, for now, just look at the humble beginnings of Amazon and couple that to the fact that Bezos saw the potential of the Internet as a driver for what Amazon can do rather than seeing the product as the driver of a technology.

The reason we should take note of this frame of mind is that we can invoke it at times when we are looking to embark on something. You know those times when we feel like we need to get out on our own and we feel that the 9-to-5 grind is just holding us back?

New Ventures

We tend to take moments like this, look at the global opportunity, think about where our skills intersect with it, and that's what we think we are limited to pursue. That is true for some people but, on balance, that is untrue. The greatest achievers, and the ones who make it as billionaires, do not necessarily look at themselves and say, "What is my passion?" Look at Jack Ma, for instance. Even today, he still has no idea how to write a simple program or hook up a server. His driving force was to launch Chinese businesses onto the world marketplace and he ran with that because he saw the potential. He did what needed doing, not what he felt like doing. You have to create your own passion and create your own luck. You cannot be at the whim and fancy of fate and others. Stand up to the forces that would sway you, and you will see your hopes of becoming successful materialize, just as Bezos did.

We seem to make the mistake that we have to only do what we are good at. That's not always true. Certainly, there are some people that do not have the ability to muster the motivation to do what they are not passionate about. Know thyself. If you are one of these people, then look for the passion. But if you are not one of these people, then don't just wait to find the passion for something. Instead, find the something that you can make the difference with and then fire up the passion. On the same note, don't omit something just because you don't have the technical credentials to achieve it.

If you look at Steve Jobs, it was Wozniak that did the technical work. If you look at Richard Branson, until recently he didn't know how to read a Balance Sheet. And if you look at Trump, he inherited the real estate business from his father. There is no evidence confirming that, to be productive and ultimately successful, you have to only do what you are good at or what you are fond of. You can be inspired by anything if you let yourself be.

Entrepreneur's Dilemma

This is the key difference between how we see the businesses that we hope to start, and the way that Bezos saw Amazon when it started. The vast majority of those who have a notion of coming out on their own think of what they can do and see if they can pull together. They look at what they are good at and hope that it meshes with the market. People are advised every day to find a niche that they love, and do that.

For Bezos, selling books was more of a way to take full advantage of this new technology that could potentially allow one business (any business) to reach out and touch every person on the planet. And to be able to do that, he really did want to sell anything to anybody and everything to everybody. But as with all astute and in-control minds, he knew that he just couldn't do that on day one. So, he picked books and used the perfect product to develop the technology and then launch that into new areas.

There are a number of rumors out there that talk about how he was only interested in selling books, and that the rest was about greed. There is also the other side of that coin, which says that he saw how well the books did and then wanted to sell more. No. He knew that he wanted to sell everything, and he leveraged the Internet to do just that.

The Start

Bezos set up the company in July of 1994 and began his Angel / Venture capital rounds around the same time – in fact, a little earlier. He figured on a $6 million pre-money valuation that originally came off rich to most Angel investors, but Bezos stuck to his guns in most cases. There were some strategic individuals that he was willing to alter the $6 million valuation for and make it $5 million. But he did this with his eyes wide open. Bezos has a stubborn streak that is not easily matched, and you need to have that too if you want to build something.

If I told you that the winning lottery numbers will be ABC123, would you accept anything else when you went to make the purchase? Would you be firm with your demands with the clerk telling you that you should take another number? Or if he told you that the machine was not working? Wouldn't you do everything in your power to make sure those were the numbers you ended up with? Why? Because you were certain of the outcome if you did certain things – in this case, make the purchase of the ticket with that number. You could not be swayed and, for that, you may be called stubborn. Were you being stubborn, or were you just doing what you were certain of? That's how Bezos goes about each and every decision he makes. His certainty makes him adamant about what he needs to do and he does not accept anything less from anyone, much less himself.

This is sort of a recurring theme in this book because it is a recurring theme in his life too and in the way that Amazon was built and continues to operate today.

Stubborn

You will repeatedly see how stubborn he can be, but his stubborn streak is not born out of an oversized ego. Far from it. His stubborn streak comes from knowing exactly what he wants at any given moment in time. He is driven by the picture in his head, and that picture dictates his ability to do what is necessary in the moment. There are many people I've heard of who denigrate this kind of behavior and say that he is mean or has no patience. They say the same thing about Steve Jobs and even Bill Gates.

What you have to understand when it comes to these men is that they are not tactless or arrogant on a personal level; they are intolerant of deviations in today's actions (or lack thereof) because they see that the deviation here causes a deviation in the final picture that they see in their head – and that is unacceptable.

Most of us mere mortals have a vague sense of cause and effect. We know that if we touch fire we get burnt. We know that if we eat junk food we get unhealthy. We understand the superficial aspect of cause and effect but, in the case of Bezos, he is acutely aware of the things he has to do and knows exactly how to go about doing what needs to be done to get it and then realizing that the results are inevitable.

He was not born with that ability. No one is. We have some of it, perhaps, innately available to us, but the bulk of it comes from making mistakes. The bulk of it comes from learning to pick yourself up and then getting back to what you were aiming for.

Bezos, just like the other achievers in the world, values the battle scars that he gets from his mistakes.

Think about that for a minute in slightly different terms. Let's say you knew, beyond a shadow of a doubt, that if you get drunk at the New Year's party, and there is a blizzard outside, that there is a good chance that you will not make it home. Some of us skirt those chances and we roll the dice. Those who do this, do it because they either have less than optimal confidence in their knowledge of things or they cede control to 'luck.' The Bezos of the world make their own luck and they do not cede control to anything, anyone, and certainly not to anything arbitrary.

Going Live

Amazon opened for business in July of 1995 and, since then, it has rapidly grown without much need, even in the early stages, for large-scale advertising. Conventional wisdom would have told you back then that massive advertising was required – now it's important that you put on your 1995 cap to think of conventional business wisdom back then.

If you looked at a business and said you wanted to get started, your business consultant will whip out his template and ask you what market you were going to target – and he would mean that both in geographic terms as well as demographic. If you had the unmitigated gall to tell him that you wanted to sell to all of America and the rest of the world, he would pack up and tell you that you were crazy. That's what doing business in the days that preceded Amazon and the Internet entailed.

For those of you who don't have first-hand experience of the venture capital market in the early 90s, getting funded wasn't a given just because you were a tech company – stories of tech bubbles, cheap money, and the craziness of the 90s notwithstanding. Just because you had an idea doesn't mean you got an investment. And even though the valuations of the 90s were overly enthusiastic, they were for Internet companies and not bookstores – which Amazon, for all intents and purposes, was in the beginning.

The reason I bring this up is to illustrate the ferocity of headwinds one would face when trying to be so ambitious in the eyes of Private Equity executives and the typical venture capitalist. It's a good thing that he was extremely personable and that he was in the business, so he knew people who were willing to lend him an ear.

When Amazon first got off the ground, even at the early stages, and the now-infamous stories of him banging away at a laptop, hammering out the business plan as they drove from Texas to Washington, was about raising the first million.

Without seed capital, the idea was not about to go anywhere.

Investor Pitch

When he started making the pitch and talking to VCs, and angels, and even PE firms, it soon became clear that it was an uphill battle. He was talking $6 million in pre-money (pre-money is what they call the valuation of a company before you take into consideration what the company could do with the investment). So, that meant that looking for a million dollars demanded a willingness to part with a sixth of the shares he owned at the time.

But the one thing that many of the investors that met Bezos at the time would tell you is that he was a very nice young man. They thought that he was as smart as a whip and every bit as enthused as one could imagine. Where the split between them occurred was in his opinion on where he was certain Amazon was going, and their perception of things. He, in retrospect, was right.

Well, they were both right. Bezos knew exactly where the company was going and what had to be done to convert potential into reality. What he didn't know was how much money it would all end up being worth. His perspective was not so much the tangible material but the intangible success. Bezos did not make the mistake many do – they mistake reward and money for success. Indeed, money and reward are the tangible features of success, but they are not success in and of themselves – the underlying achievement is. Bezos was always about the achievement.

The outside investor route was not as smooth, and so it ended up that he took most of the seed he needed from friends and family. He turned to twenty of his friends and family, as you will see in further detail later, and raised $50,000 a piece in return for less than 1% of the company each. If they held onto that till now, that $50,000 would be worth $5 billion (that's 100,000 times more over the course of twenty-four years.) I don't think many of the initial investors stayed that long. The company has, after all, had its share of ups and downs. But the comparison should give you an idea of the kind of value that Bezos extracted from a business that started in a two-car garage, receiving and shipping books on an old door that they used as a table. That was 1995.

By the time 1997 came around, the year they went public, this out-of-the-blue upstart was clocking in $148 million in revenue. To put that into context, the average startup, if revenue-positive, takes in between 40,000 and 50,000 in the first few years. 7 out of 10 companies make it to their second anniversary, five out of the first ten make it to their fifth, three make it a decade, and only two go beyond that. When you put that into perspective, you need to realize that the 148 million is a big deal, but it is not the entire picture because, at this point, that was just revenue and, at the bottom line, they were still in the red and burning the original investment they had taken.

You have to see those revenue numbers for what they were. Bezos saw them as a vindication, yet he also knew that they were far from getting started – at least in the vision of his own mind. You can think of it this way, the first few years and the first few hundred million in revenue were really the way to cudgel out the nature of the market that no one had yet tried to understand. There was a move toward online commerce, and there was even a prior bookstore that had started online, but the difference between that bookstore and Amazon's was that the first bookstore wanted to be just about books. They wanted to live and breathe books – like Barnes and Noble in the brick and mortar world; while Amazon was just getting started with books – they were not its end game.

***

Chapter 2 Meet Jeff Bezos

"People who are right most of the time are people who change their minds often."

Amazon is not about books. It's not about a marketplace, and it's not about merchandising. It is all those things, yes. It needs to be. But the Amazon that Bezos sees clearly in his head is about the use of technology to touch the farthest hearts and minds; to cover distance and culture and to be able to use technology to do so.

In this book, we will take a lot of real estate and build the story of Amazon in tandem with the story of its founder. Why? Because a truer understanding of a man cannot be fathomed when you are looking at his creation. You will see the meticulous nature of the man in the care he takes to smoothen the edges; you will see the prescience of man in the foresight he applies to its design; you will see the empathy of a man in the way his creation affects the rest of the world, and you will see the genius of the man in the way he approaches and solves the problems that inevitably arise on the way to success. You can even see the integrity of the man in the mistakes he makes and the way he recompenses.

He said it from day one – that Amazon is about selling everything to everybody and he meant it (you know that smiley on the Amazon logo – have you noticed how it is an arrow that goes from A to Z? – that was no accident).

Crossing the Hudson

By the time he crossed the Hudson from New York to Jersey on his way to Texas, he had already decided that he was going to set up his business in Seattle because of the tax structure there and how it would be beneficial for him as he sold to the whole world. None of this is by accident. Everything that happens to Bezos and around him is scripted, methodically thought out, and acted upon with the certainty of a soothsayer who has seen the future. The only difference is that Bezos doesn't need to see the future; he knows it will happen because he gets up and does something about it.

By no means is this characteristic unique to Bezos. In my quest to understand and chronicle the efforts and habits of successful people, there are a number of traits that have stuck out constantly from each. Every single one of the people I studied had this particular characteristic – they all knew the future – they all knew the chain of cause and effect was always precise and its principles, never yielding. They knew that the intangible inspiration and tangible effort they generated with consistency, ferocity, and certainty would yield exactly what they envisioned. That was their secret sauce.

Think of Edison, Einstein, Newton, and many more – their achievements changed the world. They are no different than Bezos, Gates, and Jobs. All of them had a vision that they pursued and attained.

For Bezos, the one thing that he conspicuously displayed more than most was the clarity and certainty of vision. But then there was also his intelligence in deciphering what he needed to do and then doing it.

It's like having an inspiration to create a spaceship to fly into space because you can plainly see the benefits, then you use your intelligence and resources to make it happen. They are two separate things – inspiration on the one hand; effort on the other.

He may not have been the first to see the use of the Internet to bridge the spatial divide between buyer and seller, but he certainly was one of the most resilient, resourceful, and enthusiastic people to do so.

At the end of 2017, the world crowned Jeff Bezos as the richest man on the planet based on the price of his company's stock. In 2018, just days before this book went to print, his position was further solidified when the tabloids and Wall Street watchers noted that Jeff Bezos is now the planet's richest person in history. His assets exceed that of even Rockefeller, Carnegie, Astor, Gates, and Buffett. Not only is he the richest man compared to all the people today, if you took all the wealthy people in the past, he is richer than them too.

Remember, I mentioned earlier that the purpose of this book is not to marvel at the richness of a man's wealth, but to understand the richness of his soul – the reason he has gone to this point and made the contributions that he did and to have touched the number of lives that he has.

For those of you who didn't know Bezos and where his wealth comes from, Amazon is just the start of the next chapter. Wall Street does not see the current calculation of 700 billion as an inflection point. By the way, my opinion of the stock is not, and should not be taken, as investment advice or stock promotion – I am talking about Amazon in the context of Jeff Bezos and how well he has done for himself from his start-up 23 years ago. You should speak to your broker or Investment Advisor if you plan on any investments. The same applies to any of the other titans of industry.

The early chapters to this point are really designed to lay the masonry for what comes later. We will build the rest of the book on the hows, the whys, and the reasoning so that it gives us something actionable to emulate instead of something hollow to gawk at.

Some of the most successful companies that you can think of, like Google (Alphabet Inc.), Apple, Microsoft, and Alibaba have market caps (the total value of all their stock at the current stock price) of 770 billion, 824 billion, 710 billion, and 480 billion dollars respectively; Amazon is 700 billion. That puts it in context with the other big names in business today. But the thing that is most interesting is that those same five companies, Google, Apple, Microsoft, Alibaba, and Amazon tell a different story when it comes to PE ratios. Now, remember this is not about whether one is better than the other or if Amazon is better or worse than the others. It goes to show the value of the company and if it is back or front loaded. The PE ratios are just the ratio of the price of the stock and the most recent earnings that they have experienced. So, let's say you have a company XYZ that is earning $1 per share and the price of the share is $10, then it has a PE ratio of 10. It is priced at ten times its earnings. You can tell right off the bat that, if the market thinks that this company has a lot of potential and that it will earn more in the future, the stock price will be bid up and, since the earnings haven't caught up, the PE will increase. If I think that all the company has to offer is in the present, then my stock price is going to be so much closer to home. Google is trading at 37 times, Alibaba is at 46 times, Apple is at 17 times, Microsoft is at 62 times, and Amazon is at a whopping 230 times.

Undervalued or overvalued is not the point here. What is, is that that stock price reflects a company that is future driven – just like Jeff Bezos has been saying since day one. He is not the kind of person to sacrifice the future just so he can take some form of stability in the present. When he stood firm with his six-million-dollar valuation, almost everyone he spoke with in the VC community said that it was excessively high. The problem back then was obvious. They couldn't get past seeing it as a book retailer – and a startup at that, years behind the Barnes & Nobles, Waldenbooks, and such of the world. No one could see the true nature of the vision that Bezos had. But that did not deter him. He did not recoil and rethink his plan. On the one hand, he wouldn't do it, on the other hand, Mackenzie would not allow it.

What started out as an electronic storefront to sell books during the early days of the Internet catapulted into one of the world's largest online retail platforms, changing the way every consumer thinks about consumerism and how every retailer, manufacturer, and business owner thinks about the commercial ecosystem.

Bezos was certainly intelligent as a kid but, as the book unfolds, you will realize that his intelligence, or as some call it his 'geek factor,' is not the only element at the core of his success. Sure, it played a part, but it was only one facet of a multifaceted life that he built, breathed, and lived. It's not just the vision he had or the drive he put into it. It was also the things that he had to do to get the public to adopt a whole new way of doing things. His ability to see a vision and to change and wrap the reality around others so that they see it too is also a legendary aspect of Bezos. How else would you convince tech experts to leave California and get to Washington to work in a garage for a startup? How else would you convince people to buy from you? How else would you get a group of people to invest a million dollars? How else would you get cracker-jack smart finance people like Joy Covey to come out west to spearhead the IPO process?

The why is in his nature and effervescent personality – that famous laugh, his unique gait and his total ability to focus on whoever is talking to him. Although you can't really tell that these days –

since he looks like he is carrying the weight of the world. But back then he was gregarious, affable, and smart without being a know-it-all. People who met him liked him, had confidence in him and trusted him. That is how he single-handedly convinced almost two dozen people to part with a million dollars in return for a sixth of a company that sold books on something called the Internet.

I have to leverage this to really make the gravity of the point of his affability and believability. One of the first angel investors to come on board was an investment group that was comprised of a few friends who had no idea what the Internet was. Sure, to us, the Internet today is something that is ubiquitous, and we do not give online purchases a second thought. Last month, my family bought almost all our regular shopping items online. A quarter of a century ago, there wasn't much you could get online as the web technology was nascent. It seemed to be an extension of a mail-order store. If you told someone it was a mail order store, they would understand. They knew that you picked up a catalog, dialed a toll-free number and then made your purchase. Those were the terms they understood.

E-commerce complicated things. To do the same thing, you now needed a computer, and you needed to make sure it had a modem, and you had to make sure that you had Internet service. So, for someone who knew about catalog orders, this was too much trouble. There was so much other infrastructure that a shopper would need to get to be able to be part of the e-commerce revolution. In 1994, America spent more than 60 billion dollars in mail-order products. The first e-commerce sale – where the item was purchased online, happened to be a Sting CD (for the younger generation Millennials – Sting is an artist and a CD is how we used to store music). That happened in 1994 – just around the time Amazon was getting ready to jump onto the e-commerce platform.

Since e-commerce just complicated catalog shopping, there must have been an additional pull that was able to make it seem profitable – if one could solve the inherent resistance given in adopting new technologies. Bezos had to eventually figure out how to make it work. And he did. And if you visit the Amazon campus in downtown Seattle the plaque that hangs there gives you an understanding of his perspective – 25 years later, he still thinks that the Internet and the technological colossal that it is, is still merely the beginning. His forward-looking view and ability to convert that into dollars are why Amazon enjoys a 230-times multiple in stock price.

So, for those thinking that it was an easy decision to get into online shopping – think again – it didn't exist, and its existing competitor was mail order. To take that and try to convince someone to part with money as an investment was an uphill battle. It took Bezos a year of trying to convince friends, family, and strangers to come up with the money. There were two kinds of challenges. The first was that he had to explain what the Internet was and how he could be profitable. This is the group of people that had the same frame of reference as his parents. They had no idea what this was but trusted him. The second group were the kind that sort of understood the Internet but were not agreeable to the 'rich' valuation. He had to manage both, and he had to do it together.

His rich valuation was not the stuff of dreams. He understood clearly that the Internet would change the way the retail world operates. It would allow for better efficiencies and reduced costs. His business plan did take most of this into consideration – but not everything. There are a number of technologies in use today at Amazon that were not yet available at the time they turned on the switch. But still, the raw interconnectivity of the Internet was enough to make Bezos realize that the significant economies of scale and the reduced cost had the effect of changing the retail paradigm, having the effect of improving and bridging the gap between catalog sales and brick and mortar shopping.

He was acutely aware that online retail had a mammoth task ahead of it. It had to make the pull of mail-order shopping that relied on hard copy catalogs, TV promos, and infomercials with the relatively static products that the online store would initially have. But what it made up for in impulse-buy books – which could not viably be put into a print catalog because it would result in a gargantuan volume of information – proved to be larger than the New York telephone directory.

We will get into the factors that contributed to all that as we peel through this book, but stick a pin in this factor as it is a major theme in his life, in the way he sees himself, perceives the world around him, and references his place in it.

One of the blinding factors in understanding Bezos is also the reason we are talking about him. It's blinding because the wealth that describes the man does not define his abilities and his character. It's blinding because the wealth results in publicity and the spread of public awareness bestows a celebrity status. As all celebrity adulation goes, the person becomes what the name symbolizes and the fantasy obscures the essence. In planning and writing this book, I have consciously taken the effort to avoid that inadvertent misstep.

Bezos is a hard man. He is hard with facts and hard with outcomes. He is extremely focused and believes in the power of thinking. He also believes that if you aren't thinking you can't solve the problem that needs a solution, and he is unforgiving in this respect.

There are numerous anecdotes of people who have heard the stories of his temper and naturally ascribe his demeanor to be arrogant. It is understandable to seem arrogant when one is focused or, to seem abrupt when one is in a hurry. Bezos is both of these things. He is focused and he is in a hurry. He is not given to the niceties that many people afford others who do not live up to their end of the conversation.

I understand that trait too well. I saw that every day of my childhood, growing up with my father. What used to drive me insane as a child was his constant inability to accept the slightest fault in others – particularly me. But as I got older, I understood that there are two kinds of arrogance in this world. One is the arrogance that tries to exhibit and instill who is boss – for the sake of ego. The other seems arrogant because it demands only the best. Do you want to know how to tell the difference? You see if they demand that best from themselves as well. If they only yell and scream at others but do not apply that to themselves, then that is fake ability and true arrogance. If however, they demand the best from you and no less from themselves, then you understand that the seeming arrogance comes from the tenacity to get the task accomplished and the job done. It turns out that, not only did my father demand the best from me, but he demanded even more from himself, and I see that same caliber of demands in all that Bezos does.

Looking Deep

To understand the man's success, we need to see it for what it is and, while his rewards and returns are a part of that, it is not everything. That wealth is certainly not front-loaded but comes at the end of choices, decisions, failures, effort, pain, and relentless pursuit. These are the things that made the man. That is what we want to learn. But I can understand that there is an insanely curious fervor that is reverberating through the reading public right now and they all want to know what the secret sauce in the money burger was. I get that. But it happens that there is no secret formula that you can follow like a recipe book and get that sauce to result in the same texture, taste, and consistency. It takes a replication of what's going on inside, inspiration from the universe externally, and sweat and toil of herculean proportions. That's just putting it simply. The devil, though, is in the detail and how you look at that detail, which is what we are doing here. But before we can look at it that way, let's get the glaring bling out of the way.

When we dispense with all the bling, we can then look at him, his decisions and his actions, without the distraction of the distractions.

Looking Past the Wealth

I get it. It's not easy to fathom twelve-digit wealth while we grapple with the various financial challenges and the priorities that we have to contend with because not everything we wish to obtain can fit within our five, six, or even seven-digit income. It almost feels like rubbing salt into a wound. But you should let that pain in. You should let that burn be felt and then you should get up and do something about it. What you shouldn't do is be distracted by it.

We are so inundated by the billions and trillions in the world's financial markets that most of us in this generation can be immune and indifferent to what one hundred billion is. There are many ways we can slice that. One hundred billion dollars has significant purchasing power. You could do almost anything with it. His wealth is larger than ⅔ of the world's individual countries. How's that for size? We are no longer talking about the ability to purchase top-of-the-line vehicles or insanely-large mansions. This amount of wealth is actually useless when you look at it in terms of what you can buy for personal consumption.

After all, how many cars can you drive to work in at the same time? One, just like you and me? How many beds can you sleep in every night? One, just like you and me. How many times can you go shopping in a day? As Warren Buffett said in a recent interview, "Money no longer has any utility for me." When you have so much of it, it ends up being useless in the materialistic, consumer mindset sense.

I remember buying my third vehicle with the thought that it would be a fun thing to have a change of cars and something that I could drive for leisure. After three years, I had driven one of them just twice. The car deteriorated from infrequent use. The same happens when you buy too many apples – what you don't eat, rots. As human beings, we only need a certain amount to survive, a little more to thrive and anything after that becomes a distraction. We need a little to leave our kids as a launchpad. But that's it. Every dollar above that point is pointless. Only the man who has nothing thinks that having billions is the answer. It's not. In fact, if you are not careful, you will indeed lose your soul.

So how do you make sense of this wealth?

The target of our awe at a 12-digit net worth shouldn't be at how many mansions one can buy, rather the amount of impact one has made to be able to amass that amount of wealth. Think of it as a basketball game. The points on the board mean nothing in and of themselves, but they represent the individual achievements that the team had to go from one end of the court and to score on the other end. That's what twelve-digit wealth means – it is a measure of the things Bezos had to solve, counter, and innovate to be able to get Amazon to where it is today. How much easier is your life that you can get online and get whatever you need?

How much easier is your life that you can find things that you can't find in your neighborhood store? How many people has your neighborhood store made into a millionaire? Huh? That's right, you read me. My question is, how many people has your local store, that some of you worry is going to close because of Amazon, made into millionaires? None. Do you know how many individual business owners have become millionaires selling through Amazon? Loads. Ever hear of the Amazon FBA program that Bezos came up with? You should check it out – it's in Chapter 5 – who knows, you may be able to find a new venture.

Back to Bezos.

Hold the Judgement

Understanding what makes the man that makes the business is what I am interested in, and I find that gives me the widest ranging tools I need to explore a better life for myself. I want to watch the game, so I know how the baskets were shot – just looking at the points does me no good. I can't take the points home, but I can learn how to score by watching the game. You see what I am driving at?

Short of being morally bankrupt and ethically indifferent, one's methods of getting to such heights shouldn't come as a surprise when they brush up against our own Utopian niceties.

Be prepared to break some eggs along the way, and don't hold it against anyone who has no qualms about breaking the eggs as they beat a path to the top of the Forbes' list. I have heard the comments and read the mocking sanctimonious judgment against the likes of Gates, Bezos, Jobs, and others. Whatever merit their argument may have, it has no place in this book. Not because of adulation or worship, but because it is hard to learn from someone while we are judging them negatively. And the whole point of this biography – any biography for that matter – is to learn about that person so that we may somehow find the secret to success.

The quantum of his wealth, while stupendous, should be viewed in the right context. When it is viewed as such, then it ceases to be purely his benefit and crosses over this book to become yours as well.

***

Chapter 3 Young Man on a Mission

"If you never want to be criticized, for goodness' sake don't do anything new."

Bezos was born to teenage mother Jacklyn Gise (Pop's daughter) and her boyfriend, who was just a few years older than her. It was 1964 and they were in Albuquerque, New Mexico. That relationship didn't work out and, since this book is more about Jeff Bezos rather than his mother, we are not really going to get caught up with her relationship with young Bezos's biological father.

After leaving Bezos's biological father, Jacklyn eventually married a Cuban immigrant of Spanish descent who arrived in the United States at the age of 15.

Peter Pan

Miguel Bezos was part of the Operation Peter Pan – or Operacion Pedro Pan. Operation Peter Pan was an effort that was carried out in the interregnum period from when Batista left Cuba to the time Castro came in. There was a time when the United States accepted children that wanted to come to America and they did it over the span of a few months. Children were airlifted from Havana airport on multiple flights a day and brought to the US to start a new life. They were housed in Florida, many of whom stayed in temporary hostels that were set up for them and then they eventually made their way to their own lives across the US. This happened between 1960 and 1962. During that time, 14,000 children were brought in. Miguel was one of them.

It was an extremely hard time for all those children who were separated from their parents.

Miguel eventually made his way through school, graduated from the University of New Mexico and went to work for Exxon as an engineer. Miguel Bezos married Jacklyn when little Jeff was just four and officially adopted him, changing Jeff's name to Jeffrey Preston Bezos.

The Bezos family moved to Houston where young Bezos spent most of his formative years under a close relationship with his adoptive father. After Pops, Miguel was the next greatest influence in his life. Miguel and Jeff remained close over the years and played a huge role in the development and work ethic of the already intelligent young man. Between the two larger than life men in Bezos's life, it's hard to say who had more influence, but that really doesn't matter because what resulted was that there was a good balance to all sides that pulled and tugged at him. While Miguel (a.k.a. Mike) came from Cuba and worked hard to get an education then built his career up one brick at a time, Pops came from a line of settlers and, over the years and across the generations, the family bought land and kept enlarging their ranch. Under Pops, the land was a healthy 25,000 acres located in Texas. Pops (a.k.a Lawrence Preston Gise) was the Regional Director for the US Atomic Energy Commission and was a man of science. Science technology, cause and effect, resilience, and resourcefulness were all the buzz words and attitude that arced from Mike and Pops and ran right thru little Jeff. It was just the beginning.

Bezos's natural curiosity and his closeness to his grandfather sparked off a natural consequence of him adapting to science at an early age. From science, the leap to computers was not a long shot and, with his grandfather's guidance, Bezos's interest in computers, electronics, and science quickly formed the core of his character and interests. His dream of getting to know space and space travel was rewarded when he attended NASA's Huntsville Space Camp.

With his grandfather on the one hand, and his father, Mike, on the other, Bezos marinated in science and technology. This made him naturally less fearful of advances in science, and he understood, at the very fabric of his being, that science was a way to advance human betterment: from the way we live to the way we conduct life, technology was there to improve the quality of our existence and to advance us forward in the way we organize our societies, facilitate relationships and experience all this life has to offer.

The two men in his life imparted a sense of adventure in science in the young Bezos, which took root almost instantly. As mentioned earlier, he would advance the house vacuum into a hovercraft. As intriguing as it sounds, and as adorable as it seems, the thing that occurs to me is that making things and inventing new ways was just the way his mind worked. When you combine those Infinite Player attributes to a naturally inquisitive mind, the result is a person who really does change the world.

As his character developed, many of the attitudes and mannerisms that you see in Bezos today had already surfaced as a child. He was not one to mince words or to waste time with niceties. The one thing you can be sure about when it comes to Bezos is that he speaks his mind and, if you have nothing to hide, and you have all the interest in the world for an honest opinion, then you are not going to mind whatever he says. Why? Because he is going to tell it to you like it is.

You may have heard stories and read the anecdotes that pepper the web and the tabloids about how he can be so mean to the people who work with him and the people who work for him. You need to put all that aside and see where he is coming from. This is a guy who has always held himself to very high standards. This is a guy who has put his nose to the grindstone, both mentally and physically. And all he is expecting is that all those that he takes the trouble to hire should do the same. When they don't, his response is natural – it is not mean, it's just direct. Bezos does not know how to be mean, and he has no time to be nice. He just wants to get the point across, and he has learned, over time, and from natural instincts that most people remember, not to be stupid when you yell at them.

Have you ever heard the saying that "nice guys finish last"? There is a reason for that because nice guys aren't really nice at all. They are demure. Nature is rooted in a lot of insecurities and misplaced allegiances. From the perspective of being a nice guy, Bezos fails miserably. He is, however, a good person; someone you would want to have in your corner, regardless of his wealth. Not being a nice guy just shows the level of confidence he has in his own vision. When he was 18, he had an aversion to cigarettes and understood the effects of it. Bezos is not necessarily a health buff, but he does take his health seriously, and he thinks that health is just one of the factor inputs into a person's path to success. His logic is simple. To succeed, you first have to be alive and to be alive and work for success you have to have zero distractions – and health problems become major distractions. Cigarettes lead to health problems, so he has no time for them.

When he was a kid, he had already formed his opinion of smoking and he tried to impart this understanding to his grandmother who was a smoker, but his enthusiasm and earnestness on the matter, which can come across as nasty and tough, made his grandmother cry, instead of getting her attention.

It was not something he expected, neither was it something that he relished since he did love his grandmother tremendously. Bezos remembers the lesson his grandfather gently imparted to him in the wake of that incident: "Jeff, one day you will understand that it is harder to be kind than to be clever."

He apparently has that 'problem' still today because society's definition of kind and his momentum of purpose seem to come to a head each time they meet. He doesn't seem to have time to play or be nice. But he does not mean harm or ill to the person – he really just does not have the time.

In understanding him and his ways, it took me some time to reconcile this and tee it up to the successes that he has made. What I found is that his not being nice and his success are intricately related. Putting aside all that about 'last guys finishing last,' you have to understand that opportunity doesn't wait for you as you gently step around an obstacle. You have to shove your way through, and I mean that as much literally as I do figuratively. A lot of clichés come to mind: "time is money" and so forth. But the actions that Bezos takes are ones that are deliberate and well planned. All he needs is to think about how to execute that plan and then do so. He certainly learned that from his Pops and Mike.

Ranch Life

Bezos spent his early years between the family's home in Houston and his grandparents' ranch in Cotulla, 80 miles south of San Antonio where he operated equipment and castrated bulls – one of the many things that Pops did around the ranch himself instead of calling in expert help. It must have been an amazing experience to do things for yourself.

I can't even get the lawn trimmed.

Bezos spent most of his summers between the ages of 4 and 16 there with his grandfather, busy working on the farm and tinkering in the toolshed. That mechanical side of him was something that he had even as a toddler. There is a story in the archives about him and how he used a screwdriver to take apart his crib when he was just a toddler.

Resources

Mackenzie, his wife of 25 years, sees that as a plus because she had no problems letting their kids, even when they were less than ten years old, to handle power tools. According to both husband and wife, they would rather live with a kid that lost a finger than a kid who does not know how to be resourceful. I don't know if I am of the same opinion when it comes to my kids, and maybe this is one area that I would disagree with, but I do see the merit.

What I find telling about this whole thing is that, in the silence of his meditation and the reflection of his mind, as well as the recounting of their efforts, the Bezos really ascribe a huge part of their abilities and their achievements to being resourceful, and they want to make sure their four kids do not lose out on that.

You can tell that even Bezos himself and Mackenzie see eye-to-eye on a lot of things. You can't forget that she has had a front-seat view of this entire Amazon drama as it unfolded a year after they married. She has also given unparalleled grounding influence and rock-solid support for the man that came face-to-face with so many crucial and critical issues during the development of Amazon.

On a side note, I can only imagine the conversation they must have had in the car as they drove from New York to Seattle.

Let's get back to his younger days.

The Awkward Years

You could just tell that this kid who did well at science fairs and projects was the kind of kid that tinkered with the electronics he could find and the tools that were lying around. With Pop so handy at the farm, and Mike who had built a career in engineering, he was surrounded by men who were good with their hands and mechanically inclined.

Bezos would play with electronics as young as nine. He loved the way the electronics could be calculated and predicted and then eventually, as they got more sophisticated, he could even program the once simple electronics that he played with. He even managed to build an electronic access/denial system for his room so that his brother and sister could not come in when he wasn't around. He certainly loved his privacy even from a young age, and there are miles of papers dedicated to the stories of him being a privacy hound. I am sure all the media attention he gets is the one downside that he sees to the rise in his net worth.

Among the other things that he invented along with the intruder alarm was a cooking apparatus that worked on solar energy, an approximation of a flying vehicle, and numerous attempts at a robot (more on this later). Funny how our youth has a bearing on our adulthood. Everything he played with as a kid, he is playing with as an adult now. Not only does Amazon use robots (more than 15,000 of them in Amazon's warehouses), he even builds space vehicles for travel at Blue Origin.

Age of Computers

He arrived at his teenage years just as computers were hitting the collective consciousness of the country. Bill Gates's DOS and the IBM PC hit stores in 1981, just as Bezos turned 16. Of course, the Internet was nowhere near the public eye, but the use of heavy mainframes and large computers connecting directly to each other using telephone lines was already underway.

In high school, Bezos started to learn about mainframe computers and it so happened there was a company in town that donated its excess mainframe time to the school. No one in the school felt that they knew anything about it, so Bezos pulled the manual and, with a couple of friends, he got to work on it. His industrious nature was also the characteristic that allowed him to advance himself. But the one thing that Bezos was not up for was mundane work.

Mundane vs. Reasoning

Of course, someone's got to do it, and God Bless those who do but, when it comes to Bezos, he couldn't do the things that fall under the category of minimum wage. He strongly felt that it was a waste of his brainpower and his time. When he was in high school one summer, instead of heading to Pop's ranch, he managed to get a part-time job at McDonald's and hated every mundane minute of it.

Within a few days, he quit and started up a summer camp where he charged $600 per kid for a 10-day event for 4th, 5th, and 6th graders. It was called the Dream Institute. Dream stood for Directed REAsoning. Two of the six who enrolled were his brother Mark, and sister Christina. Pretty interesting that he considered reasoning to be a skill that needed teaching and that it was something that parents should get their kids to attend. $600 back in the 70s was quite a bit of money.

When you look at the core concept of the camp, it gives a little insight into the way he thinks – with reason. His powers of reasoning are superior to most, which is the way he arrived at the valuation numbers that he did and the reason the investors that came in at the initial round agreed to the kinds of valuation that he calculated.

When he went in for the second round of funding – this time for 8 million dollars, he had two highly-rated private equity firms willing to come in. He made the choice of who would invest, and it was Kleiner Perkins – now known as Kleiner, Perkins, Caufield, and Byers. In the end, his reasoning and inspiration were the reasons he was able to build the company up to a point that facilitated an easier second round of funding before the IPO, the following year.

Not only does his ability to reason make him a powerful negotiator, but it makes him a powerful problem solver too.

Coming back to that summer.

As part of his course, he offered literature and science. For reading, they were assigned parts of *The Lord of the Rings, Dune, Watership Down, The Once and Future King, Stranger in a Strange Land, Black Beauty, Gulliver's Travels, Treasure Island, Our Town, The Matchmaker*, and *David Copperfield*.

The science component included space travel as well as the use of fossil fuels, fission generators, and other forward-looking inventions. The letters that all the parents got that year described the programs as "emphasizing the use of new ways of thinking in old areas." Funny how that is exactly what Amazon is today – mail order using computers.

Like I said, we can see the silhouette of a man when you see the boy. And you could certainly see the glimpses of what he could do with all the intelligence and that propensity to put in the effort. He was not afraid of a little hustle, and he was not afraid to bring his mind and his back to bear. He just didn't want to spend his time doing mundane things without the prospect of a future.

The thing that becomes evident as you thumb through the catalog of events, ideas, and disappointments in his life is that he has a work ethic that you do not easily find elsewhere, not even along the corridors of the Ivy Leagues and in the towers on Wall Street. The work ethic that Bezos cultivated and made second nature was something that allowed him to labor through the details and see through the bumps. There is no other way to make it to the top. There is no stopping or pausing; there is no time.

Role Models

When you want to understand the motivations of a man, you should look at his role model(s) as a kid. The one thing most men do not realize is that we all look to our role models when we are kids and the tenacity we do that with is under the surface, but extremely powerful, nonetheless. For those of us who have fathers we see often, we latch on to every action, word, and style that we can, and mimic it as the way to guide us. That's internal – we all learn from mimicking.

For boys of single-parent families, they take on a large part of their mother's strength and their mother's innate empathy. For some, the guidance comes from TV, outside friends, relatives and so on. Wherever it eventually comes from, the one thing that you should know is that it has to come from somewhere. For Bezos, it came from his grandfather and his father.

The development of a man is best narrated by the anecdotes of his life. But not everything can be chronicled, for the mundane might render the necessary obscure.

With that in mind, in this book, we take the time to look at Bezos from the highlights of his life, his turning points, and his patterns, in hope of understanding the path and the tools necessary for success.

As I observe his childhood, it repeatedly occurs to me that young Bezos is nothing short of an arduous achiever, whether it was his kindergarten projects, his grade-school homework or his high-school term papers. He was full of useful energy that he plowed back into himself as an investment.

At every turn of his childhood, his teachers recall, in retrospect, that Bezos was different – and not in a weird way. You know how some of the geeky kids can feel strange at times. Yes, they know it all and can recite a string of facts, stopping only to catch their breath, but they don't get the nuance of things or their deeper effect. Bezos differed in that he was not like that at all. He knew his stuff, but he could also be cool about it and not seem like the know-it-all.

He was valedictorian of his high-school class, and a double major at Princeton, graduating with honors and that can't be taken lightly on its own. Sure, a lot of people do well in high school and go on to secure an Ivy League education, but something was here different.

Boundless Energy

He couldn't leave things well alone; he would always go out to make things more than they were originally designed to be, like when he tried to make a hovercraft from the vacuum cleaner in the garage in his parent's home. There were many other instances of things that he would do as a child that had the earmarks of great intelligence coupled with that boundless energy and what always resulted was fireworks.

It was that boundless energy that propelled him through the down times at Amazon. And as anyone who has started a business could tell you, getting the inspiration is just half the picture. You have to hustle and jive to get the vision to materialize. You either have one of two things that you need going for you. You are either super smart and know everything about everything, or you know how to go out and hire the people that you need to do the job that you can't already do. And even if you did know how to do it, you can't do it all. You need someone to do some of it for you and, since you can't micromanage that person, you need someone to be as smart as you.

That's the thing Bezos looks for in his employees, and that is what he was looking for on day one. He understood computers, and he understood the electronics of the game, but he didn't have all the programming skills to put a database and a website together, So, he had to hire the talent to do so.

Delegate

Delegating came easy to young Bezos. Even on his grandfather's farm, Bezos learned to do the tasks that were delegated to him and delegate the tasks that he was not able to do. But he never stood on the sidelines watching while others toiled. He was always in the thick of things, doing what needed to be done and watching with a careful eye of what more could be done without the absentmindedness of a person not in the moment.

At that age, it was Pop's resourcefulness that guided Bezos to the point where there is nothing he thinks can't be done.

Of course, you would think that way too if you grew up watching your grandfather managing the entire farm on his own with little help, and the help that he did get was that of unskilled labor. But most of the heavy thinking came from Pops, who was a deeply resourceful and independent man.

It's funny stories of Pops that litter the Bezos string of anecdotes and, when he tells these stories, there is a twinkle in his eye that accompanies his guttural burst of laughter. One such story of resourcefulness was the time Pop had ordered large farm equipment at a significantly discounted price and had to work on it himself to get it up and running. When they got to it, they figured they needed a crane to hoist it, but they didn't own one. Instead of spending the money to rent a crane, Pops took a couple of days to fashion a hoist from tools and stuff he had, managing to get the equipment off the ground. This was not a one-off. Working out on the farm, far away from conveniences, Pops could handle just about anything once he decided he needed to.

That sort of exposure proved to be invaluable for Bezos and he really began to see things in the same way and work at the impossible in the same way as well. It's hard for most of us that grow up with all the conveniences that we take for granted but, with folks who have to put their noses to the grindstone day in and day out, you find that there is very little that you can throw at them to get them flummoxed.

Pops would undertake these large projects around the farm and he would carry through each one of them regardless of how daunting they might prove to be.

Bezos unabashedly admits that his lessons in resourcefulness came from Pops. That's a good thing because, if you want to make a business go from startup to the top of the world, that would be exactly one of the things that you need. Pops even had to birth cows and suture animals on the farm when needed because the closest vet was too far away. How many of us would do what needed to be done no matter how complex or how undoable it seemed in the beginning. If you are exposed to this kind of ethos then, in time, that grows, and you do all kinds of things to make sure that the objective and not the task is what gets done. And that is the reason that Bezos is the way that he is. There are stories from within Amazon that talk about his ability to focus on outcomes and achievements rather than focusing on tasks. He is not the typical manager that wants to focus on how you get something done; rather he wants to focus on getting it done.

There are tons of business owners who do not look at the objective of the action and look at the processes instead. We fail to understand that, to be innovative, you need to be resourceful; to be resourceful, you need to be results-oriented. Being task-oriented has its place, but that place is certainly not where you need to be if you are trying to build the world's biggest retailer.

The Graduate

Upon graduation, he joined Fitel, where he hung his hat for two years and invested the kind of zeal that is shown by people who own startups. His coding and attention to detail were so exemplary that he was quickly promoted and placed in charge of responsibilities that required him to travel once a week to London, from New York.

It was a huge leap in responsibility but it was one that runs you ragged after a while, and the kind of toll this exacts on a person is not the same kind of toll that a person building a company experiences. This is the kind of exertion that doesn't amount to much and so the whole thing got really old, really fast.

He decided to quit, even though he was employee number 11 and his prospects would have been good if the company made it in the future. After all, this was the company that he gave up the likes of Bell Labs and Intel for.

He quickly found employment at Bankers Trust in New York. It was a different industry but, nonetheless, it added to a skillset that was already diverse at the young age. He was selling software to the bank's clients and, though he managed to put in two years, he found that it wasn't going where he wanted it to either. He was happy to be working with software and he was happy that it was a strong company, but the x-factor was certainly not present.

He was highly focused and knew what he wanted but was not arrogant enough to let the world pass him by without him taking a taste. He started passing his resumes out to headhunters, with the explicit instruction that he was looking for a technology play.

Sometime later he got to know about D.E. Shaw with the warning that it was nothing that he was looking for. It was a new (2–3 years old) hedge fund founded by another computer scientist. Bezos took the meeting with David Shaw, the founder, and they hit it off. Bezos joined Shaw for the simple fact that he thought Shaw to be his intellectual equal and that was not something that he saw in many others.

It was now 1990, and Bezos was a young 26-year-old.

At D.E. Shaw, two things happened that changed his life forever and are, to this day, a very large part of his life. The first is that he met and married his wife, Mackenzie, and the second is that he struck on the idea for Amazon.

It's hard to fathom a rise equal to what Bezos accomplished at Shaw. He did his work superbly, and he was noticed for it. When you have someone like Shaw himself thinking that you are an amazing find, that's not usually off the mark, considering that Shaw himself was one of those left-brain-right-brain personalities who was both artistic and scientific all at once – just like Bezos.

By the time the middle of 1994 rolled around, Bezos had clocked in four years at Shaw; he was a year into his marriage, and he was sitting high on Wall Street. The thing you need to know about Wall Street and the firms there is that the biggest part of the year is around Christmas bonus time.

Bezos had already been there for some time, Shaw was doing well, they were already halfway into the year, and bonus time was not too far away. Oh, and let's not forget, he was a family man as well by this point. Then, out of the blue, Bezos finds the opportunity to open a bookstore on this new thing called the Internet. Right there in the middle of all this, he ups and quits his job, flies down to Texas, borrows a car from his father and drives to Seattle with Mackenzie.

He was 30. Mackenzie was 24, their marriage was a year old, and they threw off their bonuses and hitched their 'trailer' and rode west.

Bezos and Women

From high-school valedictorian to Princeton commencement, Bezos had the stable basics that made him a reliable young man those around gravitated toward. The physical characteristic that dominated his persona was not his height, build, or his receding hairline at that time, but it was the gesticulating and guttural bursts of laughter. You could not help feel the gregariousness of character and the fullness of life that he displays when he gets into one of his laughs. It was, in fact, the very first thing that attracted Mackenzie Tuttle to Bezos. She could hear his laughter through the walls at D.E. Shaw.

Before Mackenzie, Bezos – after all a man like the rest of us, even if he does go about it in a way that is different – created a system to meet women. Though he may have had better luck if he was as buff as he is today (wink).

Getting dates was more a science for him than something organic. The typical guy would head to the bookstore, coffee shop, or club; Bezos took ballroom lessons so that he could (in his words) increase his 'women flow.' I am sure that there are some of you who would have thought of that but, as for me, it would have never crossed my mind.

Chapter 4 Launching Amazon

"We can't be in survival mode. We have to be in growth mode."

Amazon was not always the super company that it has turned out to be. You see in the age of the Internet and in the run-up to the Internet bubble in the 90s that the paradigm had shifted from solid bottom-line financials to lofty top-line projections. At a time when valuations were given to technologies that had yet to show revenues, much less profits, Amazon was booking in revenues at levels that Bezos knew they deserved.

When Bezos set out to build Amazon, the thing that he said he relied on the most to get through hard times was the kind of resiliency that was instilled in him as a kid. His Pops was the source of that lesson as well, and he learned it alongside the lessons on resourcefulness.

He also learned that objectives superseded all other events. If you want to do something, you do it before you set out on doing anything else. And if you start it, you are not done until you succeed. It was the Edison-esque qualities of his grandfather that addressed the seemingly Herculean efforts that were undertaken during the course of events that Amazon experienced over the course of its development.

Take, for instance, the way that Bezos raised the first million. It required consistency, resiliency and, even though he gave himself only a 30% chance of succeeding with Amazon, he put 300% into it to make it work. In contrast, if you look at the typical entrepreneur today, if they think that they are going to succeed, then they put in 70%. If they think they won't succeed, they only put in 25%. Guess what happens when you do that? At 25% effort, you end up not getting anything except wasting the effort and the energy that you put in. Remember that the human body is designed to survive. It will hold on to energy, keep playing it safe and never set foot over the horizon of the mind. But to succeed in life and to build billion-dollar companies, that is exactly what you need to do. So, people like Bezos and the rest of the achievers subconsciously expand their minds and go beyond mere survival in deciding to thrive.

Most people don't do that. When he went out to raise that million, it took him the better part of a year to put it together. But for every eventual investor who agreed, there were three who declined for one reason or another. Mostly it was because the risk-adjusted valuation was beyond their appetite.

Sometimes, I wonder how those guys who passed on Amazon bear to watch the ticker and see AMZN go past.

Bezos wasn't really trying to build a web store that looks exactly like a retail store, with a customer display area in the front and a large warehouse of goods in the back. That's not really the model that has come about in this exercise. He was looking to build something that would cater to the droves of people that were getting on the Internet. It's like the old real-estate adage – "Find out where everyone is going and get there first." That's exactly what Bezos did here. The only difference between Bezos and us was that he actually got up and did it.

Pops taught Bezos how to use whatever you have in front of you to make something that your mind can see in the moment. He taught him that all things are fungible and that fungibility can be deciphered if you use your cerebral resources.

Bezos is a great fan of thinking, and he is of the school of thought that relies on the mind more than the collective – quite the departure in philosophy from those of his generation. Which is probably what makes him such a unique case study.

Distractions

One more thing that makes him unique and that comes from his grandfather as well is that, from a young age, he was thought to ward off distractions. That's why, when he talks to you, you know for certain that he is talking to you. That is also the reason he is never distracted by his phone or why you really need only to tell him something once. He is present when the event is happening and doesn't 'arrive later' when you say something that jars him out of stasis. It is a time saver – according to him and according to Pops.

I have seen this characteristic in many of the successful people I have studied. All of them, without exception, be it successful politicians or titans of technology, are always in the moment. They are always alert, and their mind is in the place and time they stand. Bezos was the same way as a kid and teachers that he impressed along the way bear testament to this.

His teachers relate stories about how they never really thought he would be a titan of industry, but they were impressed with his ability to be confident and to be able to compete with ferocity in whatever he undertook – whether it was academic competitions, projects or debates. He could talk his way through anything but not in a smarty-pants-con-man sort of way. He was born to convince people of things that only he understood.

For Bezos, what he sees is not just the product of his inspiration, it is also the product of his intellect putting two and two together. He didn't just trip and fall onto the combination of retail, books, and the Internet.

In high school, his teachers remember him to be someone who had boundless cerebral and physical energy. He would zip around getting things done, yet he would always be grounded in his efforts. There used to be a simple happiness about him that matched his generous laughter and his broad smile

Most of us find that there is a wall between what we are inspired to do and what we eventually do do. We can always see the summit but are oblivious to the side of the mountain. It's also the same when we see the wealth someone has achieved but, for some reason, we forget to appreciate the work that went into it.

There is also a loss of appreciation for the work that goes into the ambition, as well as the reality, the outcome, and the toil. We all have loads of ideas and have plenty of dreams, but only a few of us actually go out and do something about them.

We hear over and over again about how the stars lined up for Bezos, but we need to understand how each crucial step demanded an answer from him and, when we are faced with things like that in our life, how do we respond?

Take, for instance, his time at the New York hedge fund D.E. Shaw. By the way, while he was there, he rose rapidly among the ranks and was the youngest Senior VP in the history of the company. That is also where he met his wife, Mackenzie. While he was at D.E. Shaw, the Internet was beginning its growth and the company was looking for opportunities to invest in – after all, they are a hedge fund. He was making good money and was riding a good career track. Think about it: within a few years of graduating he was already at the VP level on a Wall Street firm, he had just met his wife to be, and he was living the life most Ivy League graduates dream of and achieve.

Then take that event and look at the fact that he graduated Princeton – which means he didn't really need to go knocking on doors to find the dream job. Ivy Leagues have recruitment events for seniors and offers usually come piling in before graduation. It was the same for Bezos, who had received offers from Intel and Bell Labs. But he turned them down and instead joined a startup called Fitel.

Put yourself in his shoes, with all that stability and the possibility of a family in the future. Why would he decide to leave it all behind to jump into a pool of the unknown? It's one thing if he was getting offered an MD position at Goldman Sachs or something, but he was going from a VP, on track for more, to jump-starting an idea that no one had thought about.

Now that you have that picture in your mind, think about how you would act, especially when you do not have the benefit of hindsight. Is it possible he had the vision to do it? Or was he just stark raving mad? Bezos was always a trailblazer, and that's what trailblazers do. They don't jump on a train because they have the foresight of where that train is going, they jump on that train and drive it to wherever they think it can go.

With someone like Bezos and for most of the entrepreneurs who make it to this level of the game, their starting objective is almost never about the reward – it's about a fulfillment that occurs at a deeper level. When you speak to Bezos, you will hear the passion he has in his voice for all the things that he is doing with Amazon and through Amazon. That's when you start to get an understanding of what it means to be someone who builds something that is larger than life and how he could chisel a marketplace of over 300 million people.

It's hard to do something this big when you are focused on trivial rewards. For something to get this big, it is about something so much more. It cannot be about the reward because, if it was, at the first sign of trouble, he would have either gone back to the drawing board or thrown in the towel.

Bezos was playing the infinite game not the finite one. If he was looking for the reward, the best path for him to take would have been the one he was already on. Just remember that he left a pretty secure job to dive headfirst into a startup company within a nascent industry of e-commerce on a platform called the Internet that most people didn't know existed.

Bezos talks about the early days of the Internet in a way that puts it in perspective. He tells us that, in the very beginning, he needed to raise a million bucks and he had to get the money together or else Amazon would have ended before it began. He struck a deal with a diverse group of 20 investors for the money and, in return, gave them 20% of that company. Each person ponied up around 50,000. That 20% is worth almost $90 billion now.

There are rumors that talk about how driven Bezos can be and how his employees pay the price for his drive. On the one hand, there are many who see Bezos as a 'slave driver' while to others his tenacity is just part of his charm. Well, in my opinion, you can't make an omelet without breaking a few eggs. To be able to drive your team to excellence is not just about campfires and awards, you must transmit drive by contact. For those who have no drive of their own, another person's drive can be hard to accept, and that's typically where the friction arises.

When Bezos looked at the mail order industry, two things popped out at him. The first was that he was already in the specific frame of mind required to merge the concept of mail orders to the concept of the Internet. It was an inevitable mash-up. It just needed people like Bezos and some of the other titans of industry to turn the vision into a reality.

The idea was not for the giant that Amazon is today. Instead, the idea was to merge old industry with a new facility. That was the purpose of running through the mail-order catalog and seeing what would fit. But his nature of being laser-focused was already on full display here. He didn't decide to take the entire mail-order catalog and make a company out of it; he decided to just focus on books, simply because it was at the near-bottom of the list. We discussed this earlier.

You see a lot of Bezos in the way Amazon came about and in the way it runs today. The best biography of Bezos is the contents of Amazon's history. By starting up with books, Bezos's goal was to be able to ship things anywhere in the US and around the world so, for that, he had to choose something that could be easily mailed. Books worked out great, and the upside was there because the reason it wasn't doing well in the mail order business is that there were just too many titles to make a decent collection. So, the point is that the strength of the Internet and the computer could be brought to bear on an existing endeavor. By putting in all the books he could find (randomly settling on the one million number) he created a store that would sell books alone.

Unlike today, almost two decades into the new millennium, the late nineties did not have apps and software that you could pull off the shelf and create a company. So, Bezos had to get together with a software designer to build a place where he could catalog the books and people could make the purchase.

It took fifteen months of work to get the website ready. Employee number one, Shel Kaphan and number two Paul Davis were winging it during the first few moments of Amazon's beginning. The net was there and web pages indeed had sprung up, but no one really knew how to make the most of them.

Bezos is the kind of person to jump into things whether he knows the technicalities behind it or he doesn't. He is driven more by the vision in his head than by the arsenal in his inventory. The idea is to get started and then do whatever is necessary to make it happen. But once he gets started he goes full tilt.

However, don't get the idea that anything he does is random. Just because he gets started and then works out the details, that doesn't mean he doesn't think about his actions. Take, for example, his decision to move to Seattle and set up Amazon there. That idea was because the US Supreme Court had ruled two years earlier in Quill Corp vs. North Dakota that there would be no sales tax collected from a company that didn't have a physical presence in the state the sale was made. Bezos narrowed his choices down to Nevada and Seattle, eventually settling on Seattle in part due to this benefit and also because he wanted to be in a state that had a smaller population. Why a smaller population? Because that would mean a smaller part of the revenue would be paid toward sales taxes. The remaining 49 states would not be able to collect taxes and would represent the lion's share of the market. That same line of thinking persisted in the decisions to eventually set-up warehouses. The next warehouse was set up in Delaware – no sales taxes to think about; and the third was in Reno, Nevada, also with no taxes but easily a stone's throw to California, which is a huge Amazon market. Nothing in Bezos's actions is random. Everything is deliberate, everything is with purpose, and every purpose has an infinite horizon.

The Reflection of Amazon

To understand Bezos the Titan, you need to understand Bezos the person, on the one hand, and

Amazon, his creation, on the other. Any narrative that addresses one and not the other is going to fall short of the mark. It's like trying to understand Shakespeare without reading any of his works. In the interest of that, the next chapter is designed to give you a little insight into how Amazon works, looking at its most vibrant operations so that you get an idea of what exactly Bezos set out to do and what exactly he accomplished.

If you want to understand any piece of art, if you want to appreciate the content of the symphony, you have to build and understand the context around it. In most cases, that means you need to understand Beethoven from the work he did and appreciate the work he did from fully understanding him. If you've ever sat down and listened to Beethoven's Symphony No. 9 from beginning to end, you will come out feeling elated and in awe. If you then go on to realize that Beethoven was deaf at the time he composed it, you will suddenly have a renewed appreciation for the work that is deep and inspiring and be able to get a clearer understanding of the man's genius.

A man's true biography isn't in the words that biographers pen, it's in the product of their own hands. They leave their fingerprints all over their creation, they leave their DNA, and they impart a little of their soul. Just as Bezos has with Amazon.

Chapter 5 Understand Amazon – Understand Bezos

"Position yourself with something that captures your curiosity, something that you're missionary about."

Bezos is a giant in the world of e-commerce, especially when you consider that Amazon has over 300 million users and growing. To put that in perspective, that is almost every man, woman, and child in America.

For some, Amazon is a shopping mall on steroids. For others like the hundreds of thousands of small sellers on Amazon, it's an avenue to make money. More than 100,000 sellers made more than $100,000 in 2016. In 2017, visitors spent $200 billion on Amazon. It holds more than 40% of all US e-commerce activity. That is the largest market share by far.

What you must understand about Amazon and the size of the market and following is not limited to just the awe the numbers invoke. What those numbers should tell you is that there is critical mass in what they do, which drives the value of the company and the value of Bezos to that company's bottom line.

He created an avenue not just for him to sell books, but for you (anyone out there) to sell just about anything to anyone. That's what most people don't get. They see Amazon everywhere, and they see it as just another brand. Amazon is not just another brand. Amazon is the bridge to 300 million users worldwide (and growing) who, together, present a wide variety of tastes that you can fulfill. For a retailer, that is a dream come true.

The rest of the world sees, in 2018, what Bezos saw in 1994. But he didn't just see it, he actively went out and made it happen. We sometimes mistake the true value of a company, just as we underestimate the true value of a person, by ascribing a number that we can associate. It is typically arbitrary and is used to convey with limited scope how good, how great, how bad, how awesome something is, or its potential, its contribution, and its worth. On Wall Street, we use terms like PE, EBITDA, Stock Price, Bond Rating, and Margin. On Main Street, we use things like market growth, market penetration, mindshare, and market cap. For the person, we are caught up by the awards they receive, the title of the office they hold, and the wealth they possess. In and of themselves these metrics are fine. But we should not obscure our own perspective of the true contribution and worth of the company or the person based on these limited numbers. We should remember that they merely scratch the surface. Instead, we should look at the kinds of challenges they overcame, the kinds of experiences they faced, the kinds of responses they afforded. If the former could be categorized as the quantitative measure of contribution, then the latter would be categorized as the qualitative measure of contribution.

In pursuing a qualitative measure of a man, we instinctively turn to biographies, just as we turn to analyst reports for a company. When it comes to Bezos, we do both because the qualitative measure of a man can be found in the anecdotes his life generates and the contribution Bezos made and continues to make, is described in part by the story of Amazon, and also the other companies that he has created.

Take Blue Origin for that matter. He is funding Blue Origin from the sale of his Amazon Stock. In the last couple of years, he has taken a billion dollars' worth of Amazon stock – at whatever price they were at the time and then liquidated his position so that he could inject the cash from the sale into the development of Blue Origin. His last sale was in November of 2017.

Since that first year in Seattle, Amazon had grown to over half a million employees – second only to Walmart as America's largest employer. That number would be significantly higher if it weren't for the large force of robotic arms and the level of sophisticated technology and computing power that Amazon employs to run its business. Just five years ago, America's Top Ten Employers list did not include Amazon; now it occupies the number 2 spot. A testament to the ferocity of Amazon's growth rate. This has yet to include HQ2 (their widely reported second Headquarters) which is set to open this year and is anticipated to employ approximately 50,000 workers at all levels. This is also not including the worldwide expansions that Amazon has planned for some of the overseas operations and another 50,000 across its currently existing facilities. When it is all said and done, not only will the headcount pass the 600,000 mark, but it will also include a higher number of robots and automation to keep up with its rapid growth and expansion plans.

So, on the one hand, you see him as a job creator in the communities across America that host the Amazon operations. But what you should also take note of is those robot arms. I know it is sometimes overwhelming to peer through all the different ventures that Bezos penetrates into, but there are significant numbers of them and, while we won't touch on all of them, I will highlight those that have reached a certain threshold of interest.

Robot Arms

Remember all those things that Bezos built when he was a kid – the electronic gizmos and intruder alarms, solar cookers, and stuff like that. Well, among them there was a distinct interest that young Bezos had harbored from all his Science Fiction books – it was the robot. He was fascinated by the robot and the electronics, computing, and technology that went into it. Remember too, that Bezos is an electrical engineer by training which gives him insight into the hardware. Alongside his electrical engineering degree, he has a computer science degree also, so he also understands the coding and software side of technology. Put these together with his interest in robots as a kid, and what you get is a man that scoops up one of the world's leading robot arm/automation technology companies.

They bought it, then renamed it Amazon Robotics. But at its heart, it is a company that is rapidly developing factory automation and logistics streamlining in a way that is revolutionary. The reason you don't hear so much about it in the news is because, as large and significant as it is, it doesn't reach the levels of what Amazon has grown to become. But the essence of ingenuity and foresight still characterize Bezos, and his decision to purchase the company was not only to save costs for Amazon, but also to push the technology so that it advances the causes of Amazon and locks out other entrants. His strategic perspective keeps him one step ahead of other players, and I imagine it would take at least a decade for someone to surpass Amazon or the entire basket of accomplishments that Bezos has made in this industry, assuming he is no longer around.

The true greats – the ones who deserve the accolades and the wealth that rewards them don't just have a premonition of where to be when the market makes a run. The true greats not only know where the market is going, but they also steer the market to the vision they have. Bezos not only left a mark on Amazon; he has left a mark on retail, publishing, and lifestyle too.

Amazon is such a robust platform that not only does it allow millionaires to be minted here, but it has also created other sites that have turned into moneymakers as well – think Alibaba.com. Alibaba clearly acknowledges that the concept of its marketplace is one that observes and emulates Amazon. There is nothing wrong with that. I think mimicry is the greatest form of a compliment. Don't you think? And it worked out great for Jack as well. It was a win-win for both. There are large numbers of sellers on Amazon who take from Alibaba and sell on Amazon.

That effectively means that not only is Amazon selling goods that it stocks, but it creates a marketplace for others to find goods from anywhere and everywhere to sell on its marketplace.

There are numerous niche sellers that even go to Walmart, load up their cars with items on sale, then get home and sell that stuff on Amazon for a profit. Something like that would not be possible without Amazon.

Others go to Aliexpress.com and buy goods, made in China, for pennies on the Dollar, then sell it back home on Amazon at market price. Some of these companies in China are even willing to place your label on it so that you can create branding and then ship it to the warehouse that Amazon owns, then Amazon will ship it for you to your end customer – it is the FBA (Fulfilled by Amazon) program. Also one of Bezos's ideas.

He has taken every aspect of Amazon and optimized each facet of it so that it creates value and long-term benefits for an array of participants. He has even managed to monetize the value of the brand. Take, for example, his FBA program.

If you are a niche that uses white-label products and drop-shipping supplies, then FBA would be an avenue for you to reach Amazon's 300 million customers. If you own your inventory, either by virtue of manufacturing or by purchasing it and taking ownership, then the option to get your items Fulfilled By Amazon starts to make a whole lot of sense.

The Amazon Customer

To understand Amazon, you need to understand their customers and the way Amazon interacts with them. The typical Amazon customer can be divided into two groups. The first group is the one that comes under the Amazon Prime label. These are the customers who have paid an annual fee for priority service.

The second group of customers is the one that falls outside this umbrella. Marketing may not have been his major, but he definitely understands how to extract value from differentiating with his customer base. He doesn't spend a cent more than he has to and he monetizes even the intangible.

As of the end of 2017, there were more than 32 million Prime customers. Amazon spent $1.5 billion on shipping across the board in 2016, yet 32 million Primes paid in almost $3.3 billion. How smart is that?

What that means is that, even though the Primes are getting free shipping, their membership pays for all of the shipping that Amazon does even to regular members and then there is still a balance left over of $1.5 billion. Everybody wins. The

Primes get a load of free stuff and priority shipping. The company covers all its shipping costs and that drops straight to the bottom line. If you are not a prime and you buy stuff and pay for shipping, that falls straight to the bottom line as well.

While Prime members only represent 10% of the total Amazon customer base, they spend an average of $1,600 annually versus the other 90%, who average about $600 annually.

Amazon has been online 24-7, 365 days for the last 24 years. Part of the algorithm that is sorting out what you buy and getting it shipped to you is also studying how you buy, what you buy, and when you buy it. There is a huge customer intelligence algorithm running in the background and it is gaining a wealth of information each time you visit, each time you buy, and each time you browse. Bezos made sure of that.

Understanding Bezos Through His Employees

In the research phase for this book, I came across numerous instances of complaints of the work conditions at Amazon – specifically its HQ. I wasn't going to include anything about it in the book but then, as it started to seem that the gripes that were talked about related directly to working conditions of the cerebral kind rather than the Health and Safety kind, I decided it would be a good way to understand Bezos and his way of doing things. What I found only gave me a better understanding of the facets that defined Bezos and his ethos toward work, as well as his singular focus on achieving the stated goal.

The first thing that you realize when you want to work at Amazon is that everyone is very clear about how much work you will have to put in. This is not a regular 9–5 job. This is not where you set yourself up for life to walk in the door when your 24 and clock out when you retire after spending 30-odd years doing the same mundane task, and then collect your gold watch. No. This doesn't work that way, and I wish I had known this when I was just coming out into the job market all those years ago – this would have definitely been a place I would have thrown my hat into to be considered. Of course, when I graduated, the only Amazon that existed was flowing in South America and had nothing to do with my major.

I would have loved to work here as a kid out of college, not because it would have been easy work but because it would have been one of the hardest things that you ever do if you were coming straight out of graduate school.

Why?

Because it is run by a man who doesn't see things in shades of hard or difficult; he sees things as do or don't do. Almost Yoda-esque. There is no measure of try, and there is no measure of driving the task. It's about delivering the result that has been planned for, not the attempt of doing it.

What the general public has failed to understand about the Amazon culture, just like everything else at Amazon, is that it is a reflection of Bezos himself. They have one driving force, and that is to be the best at online commerce. And that really is an extension of Bezos himself, who wants to be the best that he can be in everything that he is a part of. If he can't give it his entire attention, he won't do it. If he can't be his best at it, he won't do it, and if he can't give it his 300% then he would rather find something else that he can do.

Typically, business consultants would look at this and say that it is too vague, you need to cut that down and focus it a little more. If you don't have the focus, you are not going to be able to communicate it and you are not going to be able to execute it. These are the guys that have no idea what they are talking about. Amazon and Bezos are not about processes and targets, they are driven by objectives and doing whatever it takes to get from concept to outcome. To do whatever it takes to get that Christmas gift to your doorstep a little faster, to get your lawnmower to you earlier than you expected, and to make your trip to the store less painful and more convenient – all the while fending off and hitting off competitors who are trying to emulate and reconfigure the market in their image.

To this end, just like Pops did, Bezos sets these seemingly insurmountable goals and expects that those he has around him can meet the challenge by applying their minds and efforts. He is not the kind of person that reacts well to excuses or reasons that something didn't work out.

But if you are about to go work for him, the one thing that you can find solace in is that he may push you till you feel you are about to break – then two things happen. One, you find it somewhere in you to make it happen and you grow as a person, or you do break and you find the limits of your ability. Either way, working for Bezos is not for the faint of heart. Consider yourself warned. But if indeed you do take the challenge, be prepared to climb as far as your spirit can take you.

**

Chapter 6 The Bezos Mindset

"It's not an experiment if you know it's going to work."

There are two kinds of mindsets when it comes to leaders in the corporate world, academia, and politics. There are also two kinds of games that they see themselves playing.

These games are not really things that we think of when we think of having fun. These are games that represent the way we approach, handle, and compete. These 'games' are more about the competition than they are about the playing.

Games describe a process of interaction between players. Buying a car from the dealer is a game. The players in that game are the purchaser and the salesman scouting the lot on that day. The game can be seen as the transaction, the interaction, and the communication. The game is intangible.

On the other hand, the players are those who play the game. They initiate the force that defines and moves the game while being the vessel of its results. In the vehicle purchase example, the players initiate the purchase and the seller agrees. When the sale is concluded, the buyer owns the vehicle – the owner of the vehicle's value – and the seller holds the cash – the owner of the cash's value. Each is a recipient of different values – values that they wanted to obtain.

There are two kinds of games when it comes to the corporate world and even politics – the infinite games and the finite games.

To play the infinite game we have the Infinite Player, and to play the finite game we have the Finite Player.

So now that we have all the ingredients to this thought experiment, let's get started and show how it all fits in with Bezos and Amazon.

Finite Players

Finite Players look at one common focal point. This focal point is that there is a quantifiable, definable, and impending end. It is either this financial year-end, this end of a quarter, this cycle – whatever, as long as it is finite.

Whatever your timeframe, there is a finite and definable end-point to focus on. These players, the finite ones, have a certain mindset that is totally opposite from the Infinite Players. When you see the moves they make, the decisions they end up with, and the kinds of choices they make typically, you start to get a sense of the way they see the game in their head. Look at the quotes at the beginning of each chapter and you will start to get an idea of the mindset that Bezos has and the kind of game he is playing. Does it sound like a finite game or an infinite one? Keep reading, as you will start to make sense of it.

Finite games are the ones where you clock in at kindergarten, go all the way to high school, get to a university, get recruited as an executive, get a few promotions, retire, then move to Florida. There is a goal at every stage, there are rules for what you can and can't do, there are mindsets to make sure you follow the rules.

Infinite Players

The thing that is part and parcel of an Infinite Player's character is an incapacity to cheat. If you meet someone who is an inherent Infinite Player, you will realize that they are the kind that you can trust without hesitation. Bezos was such a person. On the trip to Seattle, he had stopped to meet three future employees and Shel Kaphan, one of the three, just fell into a trusting relationship with him, so much so that he packed his bags and moved to Seattle. That's not an easy thing to do. You can't fake that kind of trust and you certainly can't fake it with people like Shaw and Kaphan, and each of the 20 initial investors that forked out an average of $50,000 each to get Amazon to the next level.

Infinite games, on the other hand, break the molds and have no rules except to keep the game going. You play the game over and over again.

Here is a good way to think about it. If you play a game of chess with one person and you know that the game is going to be just a one-off game and, after you play with them, you will never see them again. Would you play differently? You also know that the winner takes the titles, then you will do anything you can to beat that person. You don't care if they never play with you again after that game because the second game is not your objective. Your objective is to win the game at hand.

If you take the Infinite Player and place him in a finite game, the results will be suboptimal. The reverse is the same.

To get the best outcomes, you need to place the Infinite Player in an Infinite Game and a Finite Player in a Finite Game. When you match the player to the game, the results are spectacular. Especially if you have the Infinite Player leading a revolutionary company and his finite-player managers hitting the goals and tasks he sets.

Remember how Bezos could not find his satisfaction in hedge funds (at D.E. Shaw) – the quintessential finite game. Players who play the infinite game don't recognize rules and the status quo. It's not that they don't follow the rules, they just don't see how the rules apply to their world and their thinking. Infinite Players inherently only see the purpose of keeping the game alive and continuously progressing.

If you are a Finite Player playing chess, then you just throw all you have at the game in an effort to win. If you are an Infinite Player, then you take each game as it comes, you study the opponent's moves, you keep the game going gradually one after the other, and understand that there are higher levels of interaction than just the physical game.

There is an entire branch of philosophy that is propping up on this whole finite and infinite game. It is also one of the elements of Nash's game theory. The reason I bring this up here is so that we can get an idea of how Bezos thinks, what his motivations are, and the real relationship between him and the things that he does.

Using the Finite-Infinite Framework

But there is a more important reason for us to look into this framework. Of course, we get to understand Bezos better and we get to apply that framework to a host of other achievers but, more importantly, we get to apply it to ourselves. If you look at the achievement of a person like, say, Bezos, and you look at yourself and find that you are more of a Finite Player, then the last thing you want to do is try to emulate someone like Bezos who we believe is an Infinite Player. Finite Players are people like Tiger Woods, Alan Greenspan, and Jack Welch. Finite Players make great CEOs and drivers of goals and outcomes.

If you are, on the other hand, an Infinite Player, then you need to ask yourself the ultimate question, and that is if you are happy where you are and in what you are doing. Bezos was never happy at the few jobs he landed after Princeton. Even at D.E. Shaw he wasn't happy, and he was looking to satisfy his tendencies as an Infinite Player.

The next biography you pick up, read it with a mental framework of the Finite and Infinite game and place it in context. That will give you a better point of reference so that you can see where you can emulate and where you can just observe.

Chapter 7 - Beyond Amazon

Now, don't forget, Amazon is not the only thing that Bezos is responsible for creating. He also founded Blue Origin.

The whole point of this biography is not just to chronicle the who, what, where and when, but to peel back the layers and try to understand the why and the how. Between Blue Origin and Amazon, what do you see?

As for me, I see that here is a man that looks across the horizon and has a clear picture of what needs to happen. You and I may look at the nascent e-commerce industry and say, well, that is unproven, and we are not going to take the risk on some new fancy idea. But, that's not because we are not risk-takers, but because we only see the risk. The risk obscures our perspective of the goal.

As for Bezos, he sees the goal and, because he is an Infinite Player, he doesn't see the risk as risk; he sees it as part of the package. I've spoken to numerous risk analysts and they all say one thing clearly; that if you calculate the risk of a startup like

Amazon then, based on risk alone, there is no plausible reason to start it up. There have been other men like these in history. Christopher Columbus, for one. In his case, he literally could not see what was over the horizon, and in a world that believed that if you get to the edge, you fall off, he either couldn't see the risk or he was so brave that the risk of falling off the edge did not bother him. These are Infinite Players.

Another aspect that points conclusively to Bezos being an Infinite Player is, as mentioned a few paragraphs above, his involvement with Blue Origin. Blue Origin is a company that initially started with the building of rocket engines, quickly outgrew the initially stated goal and started to build vehicles that would go into low orbit. Their purpose was to be able to take the commercial customer into space.

Do you see any demand for people going into space? It's almost kind of like seeing if people would buy a dishwasher online 35 years ago. But Bezos sees these things because he is an Infinite Player. He is not limited by desires to fulfill this quarter's returns and next fiscal year's budgets. His vision takes a longer arc to fulfill and a greater return on any possible investment. Remember what the return was on the first group of Angel investors, who took 20% of the company in return for $1,000,000.

What about Amazon and Blue Origin? How do you fit them into this framework of finite and infinite games? The evidence makes it so abundantly clear that they almost seem self-evident. Bezos is playing an infinite game in both. So, what you have is an Infinite Player playing an infinite game. He took some of the rewards of the first infinite game that was spectacular and invested it into the second. He is extending the entire game into the future.

He knew exactly what he was going to do even when he was a teenager. For his valedictorian speed in high school, he talked about building space stations and creating a better human environment. In part, this is what he said:

"...to build space hotels, amusement parks and colonies for 2 million or 3 million people who would be in orbit. 'The whole idea is to preserve the earth' he told the newspaper... The goal was to be able to evacuate humans. The planet would become a park."

Jeff Bezos is the quintessential Infinite Player, not only because he sees what's beyond the horizon, but also because he plays for more than the reward. He plays for purpose and he plays for betterment. For people like him, success comes easy in his own mind but they are not the same standards that spectators view him with, so what happens is that they misunderstand his actions, motives, and energies.

The closest thing to thinking about an Infinite Player and comparing that to a Finite Player is to think about a long-distance marathon runner and a 100-meter sprint athlete. You have two very different people and you can't put one player on the other's track.

The marathon runner is looking for distance, and his job is to stay in the moment but keep moving. He is not interested in where his competitors are (this is just an example to stress the point). The sprint athlete, on the other hand, is constantly concerned about where the competitors are and how he can keep moving forward faster. But that's just from the outside. The point that is really at hand is that the physical build of a long-distance runner is significantly different from the sprint runner. Everything from the way the energy is managed to the muscles that develop and to the way they breathe are all different.

It is the same way with Finite and Infinite Players. They are built that way and they play that way. The problem is not the game or the player. The problem arises when you put the Infinite Player in a finite game, just like Bezos was when he was at his hedge-fund job; and when you put a Finite Player in an infinite game.

It is worse for Infinite Players because this world and the mindsets of the world, in general, advocate and promote finite deadlines, and finite milestones.

From kindergarten to high school, to colleges and beyond, the entire system is designed for inherently Finite Players because of all the measurements and valuations. Those evaluations and structures force the game to be played as a finite game, and that usually messes with an inherently Infinite Player. Most times, people are surprised to hear that a kid that didn't do well in school suddenly leaves school, drops out and goes out on his own, only to become extremely wealthy. Gates and Zuckerberg come to mind.

However, there are many of the Infinites who stick it out, and even do well in the finite environment but are constantly not satisfied with whatever they have to contend with. They either find the point in their life where they get to what's real, or they stay in the finite world and struggle in mediocrity their entire life. Bezos knew exactly what he wanted and he just sailed along in the finite world until his opportunity to play the infinite game showed up. That's why he was able to make the jump from his day-job when most people would have passed and stuck with the status quo.

The one thing that comes naturally to those who play the infinite game is the art of making mistakes. Making mistakes and not getting stuff right is something that many people loathe, and others fear. For whatever reason, they find that mistakes take them back a notch or they see themselves in the light of the finite world, so they see a picture

112

that is less than what they know themselves to be. Think about that for a second. What this does is give them the strength and the visualization needed to weather through mistakes, errors, and failures. Because to them, these are not mistakes, errors or failures, these are just the way the infinite game is played. There are no winners and losers when you play the infinite game and, therefore, you have no worries about making mistakes.

In the long-term, Infinite and Finite Players serve different purposes. Neither is good or better than the other; they are just different. But when you are true to who you are and play the game you were built to play; you extract value from your contribution. Just as Bezos did with Amazon, and just like he is doing with Blue Origin.

When you look at his other investments, you can gain insight into his thinking and into his view of the world around him. He is very practical about his present moment but also cognizant of the potential we all face. He is a named investor in a number of startups that happened around that time. For instance, he is one of the early investors in Google and was nearly one of the early investors in eBay.

His investments are managed by a company called Bezos Expeditions. Bezos Expeditions has been actively investing, primarily, in companies and industries that have strategic synergies with the interests in the areas that Bezos himself is involved in. His investments are not purely designed to maximize financial returns without strategic benefit.

His investments parallel his beliefs closely and are typically made when they have a greater purpose. His initial investment in the rocket-engine company was not just an investment but something that was close to his heart. Eventually, that investment gradually turned into something more. To understand Bezos, this is how you have to see him: there is nothing random about his actions. As with the case of the rocket engine companies, it's very easy to jump up and ask what on earth does a retail, e-commerce titan have to do with rocket engines? Well, if we look at it superficially, then the answer is "nothing," but if you look at the investment based on the person, you can see that the rocket-engine investment was merely a detailed piece in a vast puzzle in Bezos's mind. He knew very early on what he wanted to do and where he wanted to go, he just kept collecting the prices he needed to get there.

As we look at the other investments he has made through Bezos Expeditions, there are just some that should strike you and reaffirm the fact that he is an Infinite Player. Bezos Expeditions (BE) makes an average of between 5 and 7 investments a year. His recent investment in biotechnology is one of the most curious because its main research and stated purpose is to extend the length of the useful life, or as they call it, 'extending your healthy life.' That's one way to refer to a company that is doing research on aging and prolonging.

There is always a method to his ways. In the run-up to his announcement of making an investment in rocket engines, Bezos used a number of shell companies to make the purchase of land in Texas. Between the amount of land he personally purchased, and the inheritance of land that he received from his family, Bezos is one of the single largest landowners in the state of Texas. His actions, again, were not random; his purchases were for the purpose of setting up the launch site for Blue Origin and the space program. While the actions may not have seemed evident at the time they were made, they eventually fell together.

**

Chapter 8 Mindset Manifestation

"If you decide that you're going to do only the things you know are going to work, you're going to leave a lot of opportunity on the table."

We ended the last chapter talking about Blue Origin in the context of finite and infinite games. If nothing else, you should start getting an idea of what the two games look like and you should be able to see the investments and businesses that Bezos makes to get an idea of who, and what, he is. Many of the things in his life strike me relentlessly in proving that he is indeed an infinite character. Even when he is intolerant of people who make mistakes, his quips are "Why are you wasting my life?"

Now think about the psychology in that for a second. He is not saying what people usually say, which is "Why are you wasting my time?" Instead, he is talking about his 'life.' He sees his time in the context and with the perspective of so much purpose. There is so much that he knows he has to do that he is not fooling around. Most people who work for him cannot always take that. They are either Finites in an infinite environment or Infinites who are used to the finite world and are getting something they didn't expect. In either case, it is normal for those around someone who is on a mission to be unable to keep up.

That's typically why he is there, and they are still trying to make it in the world. Many of his employees attribute his nature to being someone who is in a rush and someone who is highly ambitious. That is an assumption that should not be trivially accepted. It's not about ambition in the traditional sense of "Hey, what do you want to be when you grow up?" His ambition is not really an ambition; it's about purpose. He doesn't see himself as someone who needs to dream big and visualize it into existence. He sees himself as someone who is already destined to make it happen.

How many people talk about building space colonies and actually grow up to invest over half a billion dollars into it and make it work. Yep, that's right, Blue Origin is so far ahead of the curve, that it looks like they will keep their mark and hit the first customer in space mark by 2018.

Another thing about Infinites is that they don't see things as big dreams or audacious goals. They see it as the next progression to wherever they may be at the moment. They don't parse these goals in their head into deliverables and milestones; they see the whole picture. This is exactly how Bezos does things. Most people get confused about his ability to see grand ideas and, at the same time, to micromanage the deliverables and tasks assigned to staff. This is one of the things that Infinites do, and the same thing happened to all those who worked with Steve Jobs as well. When they see the whole picture, they see the whole nine yards and every inch in-between. There is no difference in the micro or the macro picture; there is no forest for the trees, it's all at once.

He is able to do that because, as many of those around him have repeatedly observed, Bezos has unbounded energy. He has tremendous resilience in his pursuits, and he has no intention to stop. Successful people believe in their vision and what they are doing. Bezos doesn't stop at belief; he knows what he is supposed to do and he just gets up every day and he does it. Then, when he gets there, he has more inspiration to go on to the next thing. And so he went from books to everything. As the motto for Blue Origin so eloquently reflects

Bezos's ethos, *"Gradatim Ferrositer"* loosely translated to mean "Step by step with ferocity."

Most ambitious people want to get there in a single leap. That's the thing; he seems to follow the adage, "Rome was not built in a day." Unlike many of the people who have graced the list of the wealthiest people, or the list of the most accomplished, the thing about Bezos is that he is easy to observe and understand if you look at his motives.

Bezos's motives have always been clear, and he has always been open about them. He goes after each goal relentlessly, but he is not concerned about failing. If he does, he just picks himself up and keeps going.

Throughout our history as a country, and our history as a civilization, we have seen men of greatness carved from the stone of the Infinite game. Churchill, the Wright Brothers, Steve Jobs, and much more. These men of the Infinite game have all the same characteristics and the same perspectives. You can see their patterns across the board regardless of the age in which they made their impact. There are a number of people in our lifetimes that have been obvious Infinites. Bezos is but one of them.

It is a common fallacy among academics who think that CEOs and chairmen should not concern themselves with the minutiae of the company. They say that the founders and the leaders should concern themselves with the strategic direction of the company and the big ideas. They should not waste time with small matters. But that is absolutely not true and that is not how Bezos does business. He is, as they say, a hard ass. He knows all the details, and he understands them acutely. He also knows the big picture. In his mind, who could you possibly know the big picture if you do not know the details? And he is right. The reason this trait is misunderstood is that those who are typically Infinites have the capacity to handle both strata of any business – the details and the big picture. That's one of the reasons Bezos is who he is.

Bezos's obvious power of resilience comes from his absolute dedication to his purpose in life, which from as much as we can gather from his actions and words is that he wants to improve everything he touches and that includes making the world a better place. There is a sense of largeness about him that transcends everything he does and how he thinks. It's how Infinite people navigate this world.

***

Chapter 9 - A Parting View

"Maintain a firm grasp of the obvious at all times."

With a better understanding of Bezos and the accomplishments he has made over the course of the last quarter of a century and, really, over the period of his life, there are many instances on which we can look back on to understand that he is, after all, human. We can never forget that. He is neither superhuman nor is he gifted. He is by no means a prodigy.

Bezos is just someone who is driven. His intellect comes from pushing himself and from the desire to fill in the gaps. He just can't seem to let anything go without understanding what it is and solving the puzzle before moving on to the next thing. He also wants to get in the game and fix whatever needs fixing and, if it doesn't need fixing, he wants to get in and be the catalyst for it to evolve.

He just can't leave things alone – and in this case, it has proven to be a good thing.

What would soon occur to anyone who studies Bezos is that he is inextricably linked to Amazon, and I don't just mean that in a natural cause-and-effect sort of way. Their link is more than that. Amazon is almost a perfect reflection of him – focused, fair, driven, yet completely on the ball. You see, Bezos can be altogether a really pleasant person to deal with, and yet, at a flip of a switch, can be hard as nails.

After leaving Houston in his father's car, Mackenzie drove while he kept pounding away at a business plan and running the numbers on his laptop. They stopped in California to meet Shel, then drove on up to Seattle.

When they got started, it was just the three of them: Mackenzie, Bezos, and Shel. They were working out of the garage of the Bezos home to keep overheads low and they were constantly on the move – taking meetings with book suppliers, meeting with shipping and trucking agents, meeting possible new hires. There was also a lot of coding going on as they needed to set up the database to hold the millions of books that Bezos had set his sights on.

They also needed to set up the website, so Shel kept piecing that together. Not long after that, they took on the second hire and then both Shel and the new guy, Paul, kept working on the simple user interface for what would eventually become

Amazon's main home page that you see today. But remember, back then, they were just selling books.

It was not as easy to start up as one might think, but it also wouldn't have been as hard for others to wing it and get it up and running. There was a tremendous level of work ethic on display, along with discipline and belief in the idea.

Resources were tight, as you have seen, and they stretched it by doubling up on whatever they could; coffee shops became meeting places, doors became tables, homes became offices. You get the point. It's not different from what most people would have done when they kickstart a business from the garage of their homes.

The things that were different was how deliberate each action was. I can't help but see all of Bezos's fingerprints on how things were set up and structured. There was some form of irony in sitting in the Bellevue Barnes and Noble Starbucks and plotting the rise of a business that would someday soon stare Barnes and Noble down. I wonder, if the managers had known this, would they have still allowed Bezos, Mackenzie, and Shel to use them as a second base of operations.

When the time came to infuse cash into the business, it was almost touch and go at the time. Bezos, who was in charge of the business end of the idea, started shopping for VCs in Seattle. There was a sense of trying to keep everything close to home. He shopped some of the funders and he got a bite. It was a VC firm in downtown Seattle that finally agreed to take on the entire $1 million in equity, but the talks went down in flames when they halved Bezos's valuation, and wanted to take 50% of the equity of Amazon in return.

Bezos turned it down without any hesitation and all the deliberateness that you would imagine. As you already know from an early part of the book, he finally convinced friends, family (his parents among them), ex-colleagues, and everyone he knows to come together and fund that first million. They only took 20% in return.

Bezos doesn't downplay that event and is very sober about the fact, that if that million dollars hadn't come through, Amazon would have never been able to get off the ground.

Here's another reason that Bezos as Amazon's embodiment is an absolute fact. In the wake of Amazon's success, principles of the VC firm that kept the risk premium high on Amazon and demanded the lower valuation were asked about that decision. The thing that was most striking to them is that they should have seen Amazon as an extension of Bezos and not just as a basket of risk. They were certain that Barnes and Noble would trounce them the instant Amazon came into view. They did not count on Bezos's resilience and tenacity, not to mention his ability to think his way out of a corner.

The server was finally completed and the website was ready – simple, but functional, the database was also completed. Paul and Shel had managed to do a decent job of things. They turned the lights on finally on July 5th, 1994. There was no pre-opening advertising – remember this is the early 90s and there wasn't Google PPC. There was Netscape browsers and little else. No doubt the Internet was ringing up online users rapidly, with over 300% growth annually, but the infrastructure was still pretty thin. There was still a bridge you needed to cross between brick and mortar and e-stores. By the way, there was no Facebook or even the hint of social media at that time. The crossover companies needed to accomplish was the ability to get existing customers on the web to their site, or to be able to use conventional means to advertise their presence, and then get them to visit from there. A purely online play was still unheard off for the most part, and Amazon was indeed headed into thick jungles as far as the challenges to get people to key in the URL and make a purchase.

Bezos and Shel rigged the computers to chime whenever a sale was made, and it did soon after going live. Every time a sale would come in, it faithfully chimed away. Within the first month, it was getting distracting as the volume of dings increased rapidly. So much so, they had to turn it off.

By the time fall rolled around, they were doing around $20,000 in weekly sales. None of it was taken out. It was all plowed back into growing the business. This was Bezos's hallmark. Even as an alter ego, he behaved on behalf of Amazon the same way he carried out his own life. He used the money to reinvest and remained frugal. For a startup to be revenue generating in the 90s, being a tech company was almost unheard of. The burst bubble of the Internet revolution in the nineties is littered with stories of failed companies, lofty valuations on the backs of zero revenues and negative profitability. Companies at the time were always headed to VC alley to rack up findings based on a promise and a smile.

Amazon, on the other hand, was making real money and putting it back into the business. Bezos's pitch to existing and future investors was to reinvest before dividend. They all agreed. The thing about the initial angel round of investments that raised a million bucks that one needs to understand is that it was given purely on the relationship. Let's clarify that. It wasn't money given to a friend; it was money invested in a business that someone highly trusted was promoting. His parents invested a few hundred thousand dollars – the lion share – even though Mike's first question to Bezos was, "What's the

Internet?" – that question apparently was echoed by all the other friends and family that invested in Bezos. We have to be clear about it, without Bezos, that investment would not have been made. Bezos could have backed selling toilet seat covers and that first group would have still backed the endeavor. This is another reason why Amazon is Bezos.

In 1999, Bezos went to Kleiner Perkins and successfully raised $8 million in a Series A (a company's first significant round of venture capital financing). Two years later, Amazon went public at $18 per share. Two years after that, Bezos was named Time's Man of the Year. This was well deserved because Time correctly recognized Bezos's contribution to the Internet and how he had popularized the e-commerce aspect of it.

What most people do not get about the Internet is that it is a world where knowledge and commerce coexist and it's no accident that Amazon feeds off that relationship. The modern iteration of Amazon, the one that quickly ascended into being able to sell anything and everything to anyone and almost everyone, is based on the ability to get information on products and the underlying problem it solves. Bezos was directly responsible for the structure and form the Internet took when he designed Amazon and its current form.

Bezos fits both roles easily and comfortably – the role to lead and blaze trails into the unknown and to follow and learn from other leaders. That is really the mark of a true leader.

His leadership skills were not that of typical managers; it was more. There is an air of intensity in what he demands from an employee, which is by no means a one-way street. He demands the same from himself and, in fact, probably does so to a higher degree.

The brand of leadership that is ingrained in the fiber of his being is one that understands that perfection is not unattainable and that the status quo is only temporary. You can either change it to fit your vision, or someone else is going to change it to fit theirs, in which case you become the follower, and they are inaugurated as the leader.

***

Chapter 10 Philanthropy

Bezos's arc of career and accomplishment is still ascendant. Philanthropy for major achievers doesn't typically come until they start to step back from the world of accomplishment and doing, fading toward their own retirement and silver years.

There is no single standard reason for this, but it is typically because philanthropy is not just writing a check to your favorite cause and being done with it. Philanthropy is more than charity and a tax deduction. Philanthropy is really understanding what means a lot to you and understanding the cause behind the giving. This takes significant time and singularity of focus and, Bezos being Bezos, he is not the kind of person to be able to do something with less than 100% of his attention and interest.

Having said that, even though he hasn't gone full bore into it yet, he has donated to some charities over the last couple of decades. Recently, he even sent out a clue to what his eventual charitable foundation may focus on, and it looks like it is going to have to be something to do with current utility –

meaning he would like his charity to have an instant impact. Maybe not all of his charity and not right away, but the first round of his ideas looks like it is going to be ideas that focus on creating assistance that could be used in an immediate situation and in an urgent fashion.

But for the immediate past, the charitable donations that have been conducted thus far have been in areas that involved immigration, education, and healthcare.

Their total donations at this point, to charity in the healthcare field, has been predominantly in the area of cancer research as well as in the area of neurology. Specifically, the area of research that they have sponsored is one that is a new field and taps into the collection of data so that future research in this field can be more meaningful. This suggests to many research and philanthropy watchers that the eventual philanthropy organized by the Bezos family, which includes the funds coming from Jeff and Mackenzie, also includes charitable donations from the stock of Amazon that had been donated to the Bezos Family Foundation by Miguel and Jacklyn Bezos.

Conclusion

The soundbite that keeps playing in my ear is when I heard him say, "It's not an experiment if you know it's going to work." In that moment, Bezos and his actions up to this point crystallized and gave me the sense of clarity and the thread to stitch the whole narrative together.

Here is a man that set out from the stable cradle of a career in New York – the exact place that thousands of eager graduating seniors from the halls of Ivy League schools and thousands more from business schools and other graduate disciplines place their allocated bids and pin their hopes of working on Wall Street. He got it. He attained the goal and he was in like Flynn. No one would have thought any less of him. In fact, the level of his achievement was still the highest of his family. I know what that feels like because I reached the highest level of education in my family too, and there were no shortages of kisses and hugs from adoring grandmothers, exuberant uncles and aunts, and gleaming parents.

But that was not enough for him, and that is not because he was greedy or didn't know how to stop reaching. It's because he was fundamentally not at peace with all of it.

His lack of peace inside was not because he wasn't happy with what he had already achieved, it was that it didn't go far enough in the direction that he wanted. When he made that decision to jump from Shaw and set out in the development of Amazon, he did indeed see the future and the result that he wanted.

Bezos does not fancy himself to be a teacher. He doesn't think that is his responsibility nor his place. But he is the quintessential philosopher. His perspective on life and how to handle its fleeting nature are things you would expect Stoic philosophers to extol, and it is possible that he reads new-age philosophers in parallel with classic philosophers. It certainly does seem consistent if that is indeed the case, because of the way he frames the grand scheme of technology and computing with the ability to apply advances that may happen tomorrow to problems that people face today.

He is the same way with his philanthropy, and he is the same way with his delivery. In fact, he is the same way with his ideas of space travel and his efforts in medical research. It feels almost like tomorrow can't come fast enough for Bezos and that he is rushing and headed somewhere in a hurry.

As we come to the end of our introduction to Bezos and the understanding and analysis of his actions and anecdotes of his life getting to where he is, we see that the arc of success doesn't necessarily start when you are an adult. All the things that you accomplish as a child and develop in your pre-teen years coming into high-school then leading up to college serve to form the foundation that predicts where you go as an adult.

Let's be clear, we all can't be the richest man on the planet – by default, there can only be one person. Even a dollar short and you fall to second place. On the other hand, if you set the bar to achieve based on what he has achieved, then you come to a path that leads toward different levels of accomplishment. You have the cerebral accomplishment of facing challenges and overcoming them; you have physical challenges that you have to muster up to; you have inspirational challenges that you hone with meditation and focus, and you find that the moment you decide you want to get somewhere and you stand resolute in your decision, only two things remain. The first is to know that your limitations are temporary, and the second is to remember that all problems have a solution and all solutions are a function of the degree of your resourcefulness.

Bezos just turned 54 this year. That's a relatively young age, and he is still at the top of his game.

When he got started, when he made that trip across the country, he was a young 30-year-old who had less than a decade's worth of real-world business experience. He certainly had no experience in merchandising or website development for that matter.

From this one point alone, as we have also talked in the book, you can be sure in your own life that you do not need to be totally caught up on what your training is and what you think you can do. The real key is whether you are a person with a Finite Game or an Infinite one. Once you can figure that out, choosing the stories that will most benefit you become so much easier. But that is also not meant to dissuade you from reading books of men and women who are not the same players as you. If you are an Infinite Player, by all means, read as many books about Infinite Players as you can get your hands on, but do not neglect the Finite Player. Doing so further removes you from a balanced equation.

In other words, read more about the type you represent and then read about the ones that you are not. Guess what that does for you. It gives you insight into how the other half makes decisions. So, the next time you meet a person who is your opposite, you know where their pressure points are.

When you realize that Bezos is the quintessential Infinite Player, you start to see the writing on the wall and the earmarks of his actions. You start to see that he is not the type to be placed in the straitjacket of routine, but he is also not one to be concerned with processes as much as he is concerned with outcomes that are superior. Although that is not to say that he is not interested in keeping the processes strict – he knows that, in a large organization, there is only so much freehand you can afford at the organizational level before things start to get out of sync. But at the higher levels and as far as delegation of responsibility goes, solving the problem takes precedence over keeping the process.

Infinite Players essentially see the larger picture. That's why they know that life is not limited to this quarter and this financial year. It's a lot larger than that and Bezos is no different. That is the anchor that allows him to stay true to a long-term goal of constant improvement. If he were to have developed Amazon as a Finite Player, then there would have been a very different outcome. An interesting comparison would be someone like Balmer at Microsoft and Tim Cook at Apple. Neither are the founders, but the culture of the company that was left to them by the key founder dictates the culture that overtakes them and creates the parameters of the game.

Jobs left behind a company that played the Infinite Game; Gates left behind a company that, for whatever reason, played the finite game. Microsoft has always, in recent history, been about the quarter, the year or the next two to three years, at the most. And what happens to that sort of a company is that it shows in the products that they come up with. Look at the Windows phone that didn't last long because they conjured the phone up as they were trying to compete in a market they did not develop and conjured a device just so they could compete in this quarter. The result was catastrophic. But if you look at Apple, on the other hand, you see the Infinite culture becoming ingrained in every single one of the hands on deck. In my upcoming book on Steve Jobs, I dive into this a lot deeper, but the reason I bring it up here is that the comparisons are significantly relevant. The Infinite Player always wins over the Finite Player. Look at the battle between Samsung Phones and the iPhone. Samsung is fast to come out of the gate with products that capture the market's attention, and their price points are enough for the mass market to adopt easily, but then Apple doesn't rush to catch up. They bake their technology and, when they are good and ready, then release the product. Now, mind you, I am certain that there will be a number of you who are not Apple fans, and believe me when I say I am not an iPhone user, but I do appreciate the way they approach the market and the way they handle design innovation, as well as the way they introduce disruptive technology every once in a while that sets the trend for others to follow – case in point – the iPad.

Back to Amazon.

Amazon is a trendsetter too. It was Amazon that AliExpress followed and it was Amazon that the likes of Lazada in Germany followed as well. Amazon is no doubt a trendsetter, and they will continue to be. When you are at this level of the game, your job is not to think about the small stuff, but to think about how to set the trends and have others follow you. If no one is copying you, then you're not doing it right.

Another of Bezos's poignant sayings that I will take with me for some time is (allow me to paraphrase) that we are all the sum of our choices. It is one of those things that pulls right at the strings that makes me remember I am human, no different than the men I write about. No different than Gates, Jobs, and Ma, and no different than Bezos in the endowments that result in this form and this function. We are all connected; we all assume the same content of our biology. Where we differ is in the choices we make, the content of our intentions, and the consequence of our actions.

Those that stand up to achieve do so with the certainty of cause and effect. They know that doing nothing, on one side of the spectrum, results in obscurity. Doing something gets you by but doing the best of your ability gets you far.

If Bezos is indeed to be believed, and he is, then we, being the sum of our choices are a work in progress. We can change the calculus of historical choices just by making new choices – if that is indeed what needs to happen. Or we can just read about these men of accomplishment while sitting by the river and watching the grand riverboats steam by. The choice is ours – there it is again: choices.

Bezos was not happy in the jobs he took on not because he didn't like working, but because he was tired of mediocre achievement. That bell rings in all of us. We just misinterpret it, or the sound of it tolling is muffled by our fears and laziness.

We are happiest not when we are rich and famous. We are happiest when we are at peace and progressing. We are happiest when we solve issues that no one else can come close to. We are happy when we build something.

Bezos is happy not because he gets to play with rockets, robots, and technology. He is happiest because he is able to keep his mind sharp doing something that no one else can and build something new every day.

***

If you enjoyed this book, I would be forever grateful if you could leave a review on Amazon. Reviews are the best way to help your fellow readers find the books worth reading. Thanks in advance!

Make sure to check out the next book in this 'Billionaire Visionaries' series:

<u>Elon Musk: Moving the World One Technology at a Time</u>

Made in the USA
Middletown, DE
25 August 2018